SPEAK

The Night After I Killed Myself

By: Author Queen Lattifa Bryant

ATLANTA NEW YORK JAMAICA WEST AFRICA

ISBN #: 978-1-950279-06-7

Edited + Formatted by The Literary Revolutionary + Team

Cover Design By: Yemi | Crea8tive Designs

Cover Photo: Horace McKelvin

Manufactured in the United States of America

Follow the Author!
Instagram: @TheAuthorQueen
@SpeakTheBook
www.authorqueen.com

A Note from Author Queen:
This publication is based on a true story, from one survivor
to another.

National Suicide Prevention Lifeline
1-800-273-8255

Before you engage in this book, I want you to stop what you are doing and hug yourself until all of your broken pieces come together again. You're the only one who can do it, so wrap your arms around yourself and make it happen. Love yourself, first. Know that suicide is a permanent solution to a temporary problem. Suicide is a serious thing. If you know anyone who is suicidal or who may become suicidal, please get them help. No one should be in pain. Everyone should master the art of self-love, no matter how long it takes. Healing comes in waves—please surf, my love.

In loving memory of Areather Strozier, my maternal great-grandmother.

Great-Grandmother,

You inspired me to write SPEAK. I remember you having so much hurt on your heart, and I remember the sacred things that you told only me. I love you and have always loved you. Without you, I could not exist.

Great-Grandmother, I choose to speak because for so long, your voice was mute. Not many people heard your side of the story, nor did they care to listen; but I always have. May you speak through me. May I be as strong, if not stronger; bold, even bolder as you once were. May your smile shine through me. May your light shine through me. I give thanks for your life first and foremost, because without you, there is no me. Although you transitioned, your voice still remains. Thank you for showing me how to live fiercely, without regard to what anyone thinks of me. I appreciate you for being there the first time that I truly discovered that I was "a woman." Your smile, your love, your hugs will always be unmatched. Thank you for allowing me to be the last person you spoke to before you transitioned. May your soul rest in peace. May every scar that you endured be healed. May you walk with me daily. Protect me and continue to pave the way so that I do not make the same mistakes. May I break generational curses, if you will allow. Show me how to command my voice to speak to the things that hurt. May you help me in the times that I feel weak. I give thanks honor and praise to you, my gracious ancestor.

You loved me enough to set an example of what I should do and shouldn't do. Your blood sheds through my veins. There is nothing but respect, love, and gratitude that I have for you. As I give my love and respect, please give me your love and support in all of the endeavors of life.

Your beloved, "Booty Booty"

Contents

Introduction

"If you are silent about your pain, people will kill you and say you enjoyed it."
– Zora Neale Hurston

As I sit on my balcony, I realize that I, in fact, do not want to kill myself. I realize that life is truly beautiful. Life is precious and I was born a Queen. I stayed up until two AM one night, working on a dream that people barely believed would come true. I thought of who will read my book and how will it make them feel. The lies I tell myself are: *no one will be interested in it, people will judge me after reading it, publishing this book is a waste of time and money, the people that I wrote about will never want to speak to me again, and lastly, my story is embarrassing.* However, the truth of the matter is that SPEAK will not be for everyone. I simply trust that it will land in the hands of those who need to hear what I have to say. And if people judge me, that is their right and their business. I have accepted my truths and nothing that anyone says can be used to destroy me. And actually, not writing my book is a waste of time and money, because it is my duty to SPEAK.

This may be different from any other piece of work that you have read. SPEAK was written during a time when I was on a self-seeking journey in my early twenties as I silently battled with considering a permanent solution to a temporary situation: suicide. I have decided to publish everything that I wrote in hopes that if this book lands in the hands of one person to help them see their life has value, then sharing my story was well worth it. We all struggle at times, as life can be very difficult. Sometimes it can be overwhelming. Perhaps somebody reading this will also realize that they are not alone in their thoughts and troubles, which may make it easier for them to seek assistance, professional help, or have healing work done. I sincerely hope that anyone facing these kinds of demons will find strength by reaching out to someone who can help. **You do not have to face your troubles alone.**

I look back at my past experiences and my initial reaction is "wow!" I am so grateful for every time I was able to call my Godmother and have her pray for me. She saved my life on many occasions. She has always been there for me, no matter what time of the day or night. I would call her right before I found myself in that suicidal bombshell. And there she was, willing to love and receive me, as well as pray for me. She used her energy to pray for me during times when I knew that her cup was empty. From this, I learned the importance of first praying and meditating for myself. It was a selfish and unfair act to have her praying for me when I never attempted to pray for me. After all, no one knows me better than I know me. No one knows what I need from the Most High, more than I know what I need from the Most High. More importantly, though, I learned to love, respect, and appreciate people's spiritual gifts because there are some people who are truly ordained by God. Angela is certainly one of them.

I learned the importance of receiving these spiritual guides, because they often fight battles that we know absolutely nothing about. I actually did not realize how much I even meant to my family until after I announced, at my graduation dinner, how I attempted suicide in my apartment. There was not a dry eye at the dinner table after that. But there were times in my life where life was simply unbearable. I wanted to get inside of my car at times and crash it, or literally "go plank in traffic," one of the most popular sayings during college. This was my life for quite some time and now that I reflect on the day I considered suicide, I am more than grateful that I did not succumb to those temporary feelings. I know that if I would have truly killed myself, I would not have had the ability to SPEAK.

I'd like to think that those who actually go through with it, did not have a voice. Many victims feel lonely, believing that they have no support. According to the American Foundation for Suicide Prevention, in 2016, there were 44,965 recorded suicides. If it was not for the love of God, my Godmother, and my family's support, I would have been number 44,966. I speak for all 44,965 individuals. I'd like to thank my family for allowing me to openly express myself even when my voice cracked. My mother, for always allowing me to be who I am, not forcing her thoughts and beliefs of who she wanted me to be on me. When most people could not tolerate the way I commanded my voice, she always could because she knew that I was not a "child that needed to stay in a child's place." She understood that I was the Universe in motion; healing, bending, breaking, and learning beautifully. She loved me still, protected me still, prayed for me still. Her *I love you's* kept me afloat.

Thankfully, I was able to overcome, and I have a lot of people to give thanks for. My advice to those of you who are in the shoes I once wore, is that you do not have to suffer in silence. It is my humble pleasure to be there for you, because I am not only my sister's keeper; I am my sister. We can and we will heal together. We will destroy generational trauma through our voices.

I am grateful for discovering that every moment I thought I was lost, I was found. I found everything that I thought was missing inside of me. I have a newfound hope for self-love. And I am still the Universe in motion, taking one step at a time, planting my feet exactly where my feet belong. Today, I write for healing, therapy, and creative expression. I write for freedom.

SPEAK was founded chiefly on the solaces of pain and the complexities of my healing. I allowed my pain to bleed through my pen and used my healing to publish for the world. It compares a series of feelings and emotions written down in widely different moods and circumstances, at various times and dates of my young adult life. I was hesitant about writing, but I do not greatly regret this. I have consented to publish a small selection of short stories in the form of poems which may not rhyme according to linguistics but do flow in the perfect rhythmic pattern of my life. The passages in this book have been my tool of therapy and expression as I reflect on life. I am a conscious transition whose closet is full and can longer close. If I choose to remain silent about my pain, people will tell my narrative for me; and no one can tell my story like me.

Something about speaking my peace makes me come undone. There is so much to be heard, seen, and felt in those moments.

To SPEAK is to

Separate from the world so that you too can elevate
Pray and affirm yourself out of your situation
Encourage yourself and protect your *energy*
Acknowledge that where you are is not where you will always be and lastly,
Know your worth & then add tax

S.P.E.A.K.

Dear Reader,

Always respect those who hurt you. You shared time and energy with them. Be mindful how you speak on them and remember, you chose to be in their presence. When your season marks its end with an individual, be careful how you speak on him or her. What you say or think about them is a direct reflection of who you are and what you chose to give energy to. Respect your exes and respect yourself enough to not go back-- be it ex friends, ex relationships, ex managers, let it all be an example of how you purposely move forward each day without the intentions of looking back.

The Night I Killed Myself...

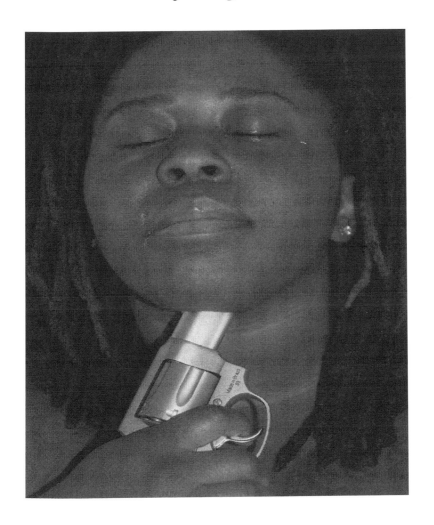

the night I killed myself
my ex blamed himself for my death
the people that loved me cried relentlessly
the night I killed myself
I regretted it.
but,
why did I kill myself?

her at 2am

these were the hours that the whispers were the loudest
she would enter into my home
majestically yielding up the God of my insecurities
she would barricade me to the floor
as she poured poison into my ears
placing all of the right weapons into my hands
so that she could guide me in taking myself out of my own
misery

by now the neighbors think i am insane
i discovered a home in between joy and pain
and i shoved my car in a garage full of suicide
i lived next door to pull the trigger on my left
and you have more to live for on my right.
but on this particular night at 2am
it became so hard for me to breathe
i wanted to die
my hands and knees were bloody
as i searched on the concrete ground
for reasons to live

my mother and father told me that i had
more to live for but those words bounced off of my ears

i no longer wanted to feel the pain associated
with being a single, bitter black woman
bitter that i allowed men of my past relationships to misuse
me as i continuously
opened my heart to them and
poured love into the crevasses of their souls

the last relationship was most toxic
but truth be told
we were bad for each other

but it pained me to stay and sometimes hurt me even more
to let *him* go
but i knew letting go was what i had to do

i could not continue being a hotel room when i knew i was
a home
but i knew that if i continued to operate at my lowest
vibration
i would have killed myself
drowning in thoughts of unworthiness because of the way
my relationship had recently ended

he almost killed me and i almost let him
i almost had my mother in all black
on the front row of the white baptist church on pearl street
mourning about her only daughter
her darling angel who used a tightrope
to cut off the circulation to her throat
all because of
him

him

when i took my first hit of him
i became addicted
and though he was extremely intoxicating
i continued to swim in his rivers of i love you

i was mesmerized by the tears that he cried for me
i never felt a high like this
in freshman year
we were a breath of fresh air
but by senior year
he became the reason i could not breathe
the two of us polluted everything

my blackened lungs were filled with clouds of him
but our love soon went into flames like a burning home
two peas in a pod
two gifts from god
trapped inside of a burning castle

over the years, we were forced to inhale the smoke
knowing that the more we took in
the faster it killed us both

see
i became his fire on the side
his mistress queen
while she put his fires out
the way he belittled me
reduced my worth
as he often came to me for pleasure
i was the one to light his soul on fire like only i could
but she had his heart
she held the torch that would eventually burn us all

—

beware of men who picture you in their beds but not in
their life

loving you breaks me
and slowly overtakes me as i
live this life of lies
how did i become so unwilling to quit?
a fool for punishment
begging for more
laying with him
playing with fire
flames
burning me alive
it seems that i have nothing to give but my body

to serve like fresh dirt for him to bury his bone.

karma can be a bitch with a venereal disease.

the escape

i sat on the edge of my bed several nights in a row
sizing up my second story window
'suicide is an individual right'
she whispered to me.
she was the part of me
that knew neither how to fight nor how to carry on
she was the one who always crept into my mental capacity
though it was often overflowing
i knew not how she always seemed to find
her way inside of my head at 2 am
"how did you get here, again?"
i pondered
where exactly did these suicidal thoughts come from?
did he leave them here?
she never answered

i did most of the talking and convincing
as she reassured me that my life was purposeless now.
"jump"
she demanded.
JUMP

suicide here
deep in my head
suicide there
me wishing i were dead
i sat thinking of jumping out of my window
telling myself that suicide would stop
the pain that he caused
and when i finally went through with it
he would realize what he done
i was willing to die to show him how much
love kills

but i knew he would probably show up at my funeral with
her
or he would use her silver escape
to drive 4 hours to visit my grave
to escape from her whenever he missed me again
meanwhile my silver escape rested on my tongue
it felt so right yet tasted so wrong
me on the edge of my bed
finger on the trigger
ready to escape the world

the end of me

i could not say a word
tears flooded my eyes
as i tried to straighten myself up
before i got out of the car
nothing seemed to work
liquid prayers as i walked into the hospital
begging god to grant me the courage to
accept the things i could not change

the automatic doors to the hospital spread wide opened as if
its facility expected me—
greeting me with a wide hug by the automatic slide door
and a warm smile from the nurses up front

"hello, how are you?"
do you really wanna know, miss?
i am injured past the point of repair
forced to enter into this nerve wrecking place
"how can i help you?" she asked
i don't know if you can -- i thought
i was mentally sick

do you have a pill that will prevent me from committing
suicide?
i thought to myself
i began to shake as the tears began to flow
i could not speak
the nurse grew slightly impatient with me
as she stamped her right arm onto her thick hips
"how can we help you ma'am?" she bellowed

time stood still for me
i did not realize that i was still silent
the sound of her voice trembled through my spine

i was already nervous but she made matters much worse
thus, i began to think of ways to communicate without
speaking
i slowly pulled out a crumpled sheet of paper from my
jacket and wrote

my boyfriend cheated on me and
i need to get tested

she smiled and whispered
do you have any symptoms?
any cold sores or blisters?
she turned me away
telling me that without symptoms,
'we cannot help you here'

I walked away

———

webster
symptom: a physical or mental feature that is regarded as
indicating a condition of a disease, particularly such a
feature that is apparent to the patient.

wrap it up

if you're reading this
tell my mom i'm really sorry
i could not talk to her about it because i did not want to hurt
her
nor did i need her to try and stop me
and i know that i was supposed to graduate college
this year but i cannot take it anymore
every woman has a breaking point
so, here is where i end it all
i am tired. and no one really cares
none of the family members call me to see how i am doing
here in these cold Atlanta streets, surrounded by sex, mary
jane and molly.
and as for you?
don't cry for me
she will probably drop you off in her escape at my
apartment complex
you will sneak around to the building and find me collapsed
on the ground — dead

this is the night i will make the decision to jump
and when you call my mom don't cry
do not write paragraphs about how much you loved me
because tonight i am here alone in my darkest hours and
you were not here to stop me
do not pretend that i was a wonderful girl and that you
loved me
you promised me that you would leave her
and propose when i got back from England
and i believed you like the idiot that i was
and today makes 1 year since i've been back from England
and i still don't have a ring
and that explains the ring around my neck tonight—
a ring from the tightrope that i will use to hang myself

i'm going to do you both a favor and i'm just going to end
it here
so if one day you wake up and i am gone
please don't cry.
this is not to make you feel bad. it is for me to feel good
i can't feel good by myself
i can feel good in my casket
whether you loved me or not
i do
whether you listened to me or not
i spoke.
whether you will miss me or not
i'm dying tonight.
because when i was alone in my darkest hours
you were not there
by the way
tell your mistress congratulations on her degree
GO PANTHERS!

a call from Angela

"are you there?"
"hello"
"Lattifa…tifa…"
click
call drops.
ring.
it's Angela.
"hello?"
"Lattifa?"
"let me pray with you."
"hello…"
"i cannot hear you but i am still going to pray…"

Angela was my only hope at 2am when i had my last straw

i listened to her pray during the moments i could not pray
for myself
i started purposely tuning out the sounds of god
because it grew hard to digest faith when scripture explains
by his stripes we are healed
but my doctor says *incurable*
the last time i prayed was when i asked god
to let you be the one for me
is this how he answers?

save me

i first got saved at 8 years old
again at 14
and somehow at 24
i still needed saving from myself
i could hear Angela's voice traveling through my cellphone
gently calling my name.
i slowly walked away from the phone as she prayed
I reached into my closet and
began flirting with more thoughts of suicide
as suicide ran its fingers through my hair
reminding me of why i should
gently placing its hands between my legs
caressing my brain
lately
this is all i could think about
with tears stinging my eyes
what do you do when you still feel empty after prayer?

the other woman

i prayed for you to be my one and only and you were
only for her
you were the same
he appeared to be everything i ever dreamed of
the let me hold your books and walk you to class type
the hold my umbrella and i'll walk in the rain guy
with elegant eyes
a nice smile
warm hands and
soft skin
beware of wolves in sheep's clothing

toxic love thoughts

i love him
he can change
he needs me
he cries
it is his past
it won't stop
i can leave
but i love him

empty

if i die i am nothing
if i live i am nothing
when will you realize i love you?
i am a hypocrite
we both made promises we both should have kept
and it is not the fact that we ended, that hurts

it is what we could have been
or had the power to be
that is what stings
but in a moment of weakness
i will come running
i wish i never met you
i would take a bullet for you
because it might hurt less than this
the sick side of me loves pain
we are absolutely toxic for each other and we became okay
with that

spiritually transmitted demons

the letter from the health department read like this in so
many words:
congratulations: your lifestyle as a sidechick has
caught up with you and this is what you get

why do fools fall in lust

i reminisce on what life was like before the letter
not realizing how reckless i had been as the other woman
ignoring my inner-self and
operating from my lowest chakra
i had no idea of how to love myself at the time
was this god's punishment for me trying to recreate his
canvas?

—

i cried until the river ran dry at how
i allowed my ignorance to overtake me
being the other woman is a deadly game to play
everything in life has a process

nothing just happens
all of the secret hotel visits
proves i cannot hate the consequence if i enjoyed the
process that took me there
i knew my role
i operated in my lane as
the low self-esteem rider
wondering if this is an std or if i am just itching
you can't hate the consequence and love the process that
got you there

dry texts

i feel toxic
and worthless
please stay away from me
let it go before it destroys us both

men will tell you they love you until they discover that they
don't

tripping

if i could go back to the day you asked me if it would be
okay to walk me home i would have said no
i was mesmerized at how you used the purple umbrella to
cover me in the rain
meanwhile you walked
holding the umbrella over my head
as you became drenched

you did not turn out to be who i thought you could be
i drowned myself in your potential
dried off in the arms of your lies
i rested in a sauna of i love you's
and allowed your lips to massage my broken vessel.
i longed for you
you were everything i dreamed of
and exactly what i had imagined.
i fell for the first guy that gave me attention

burned

consumed by the fire of love flames
i took my turn with you
i asked for it
and you gave it to me
you served me everything but your heart
the moment i thought one heart could love two women
is when i knew i had a problem
i tried believing the human heart is capable of being in love
with two people at once
you fed sweet words with a bitter tablespoon of action
but i only kept you to make you perfect
that is not love
we both speak of suicide

together
i am afraid that one of us may pull the trigger eventually

what if i am already dead?

meet up

i was thrilled the day i met her
i introduced myself to her and she would not look me in my
eyes
i approached her while walking
to my next class
i reached to shake her hand
and
she froze
"hello my name is lattifa
it's nice to finally meet you
i am the ex-girlfriend of the man who left me for you"

boys love easy college girls

i wanted to take a moment to get
to know her
and see what she was like
she appeared to be everything
he thought i was not
i could not understand
why i woke up wishing to be in her position at times
wishing that i was in her body with him next to me
i wanted to ask her how is he
is she treating him right?
what was her magic trick?
and it was at that moment i realized that her success was
not my failure

he said:
why do you always compare yourself to her?
i do not
i compare the way you treat me to the way you treat her
the way your eyes light up
the way you take charge of the camera in photos
how dull her eyes are while yours light up
taking you for granted
when i would kill to have you here with me
meanwhile you push the camera away
kick your friends when they take photos of us
telling me you cannot post me because your social media is
for business only
and posting me would ruin your career

why do fools fall in selfies?

———

the night i killed myself

i could not bare another night of crying myself to sleep
the night i killed myself
there was no other way out for me
i stood over the body, trying to speak peace but my body
was still
cold black bruises surrounded my dangling neck

there was no way to un-do what i had already done
i shook the body as hard as i could
but it wouldn't move
i tried the cpr that they taught me at training
but nothing redeemed me

i sat there, crying and trying to figure out ways to undo
what i had already done
it was 11:59pm and *he* was still not home.
i reached for my old cell phone, and it was mom
"sunshine… Joel Osteen says no matter what's happening,
choose to be happy. don't focus on what's wrong. find
something positive in your life. thank god for the small
things. i love you angel."

no response from the angel who gained her wings last night
my mother would soon learn the hard way that
it ain't no cell phones in hell

i went back to the body dangling from the closet
and i tried to talk some sense into her
i told her about everything i learned about healing
self-care and self-mastery –
placed a crystal inside of her bra
then placed the suicide hotline number in her pocket
closed the closet doors shut

and grabbed my old suitcase to head back home to tell
mother the news

i packed my bags and took one more look inside the cold
townhouse
where she once lived –
her ex-boyfriend's family were sound asleep on the
couches

i went back up to her room one last time to see if maybe he
had come home yet
but her bed was still empty
he has been out *fishing* for the past two days

i made my way to my mother's house and watched her
through the window
she sat on the floor of my room crying when she heard the
news
she was crying because i ended my life
she had no idea of how miserable i was inside
and how much i had wanted to die since i was fifteen

i sat next to mother as she clinched a collection of my baby
photos
in her palms until they were wrinkled and drenched with
her tears.
i watched her beat herself up and ask god why
i put my arms around her and i promised that my death was
not her fault

was it his fault?

breaking point

i watched him in the shadows
watched him move her into his home
pay the bills
become the man of the house
i saw his life light up without me
and i become a thing of the past after i killed myself
i knew i had only been something to do
when he had nothing to do
second place does not get a prize
you were a scar in my flesh
yet my flesh still got weak for you
how is that possible?

between my legs was his man cave
the one little room the man of the house is given permission
by his wife to do whatever he wants in it—
the male sanctuary.
yet after any holiday celebration,
he will go back home leaving the man cave in the garage
cold and neglected once more

i could be anything in the world that i wanted to be,
but i wanted to be his.
thinking of my eagerness to see the woman he left me for
what draws him to her?

i taught men that it was okay to treat me badly
until there was nothing left of me
i began to hate men and hated myself for the way i allowed
them to treat me
and it killed me knowing that i didn't know when to stop

carcass

i let my bones rot to feed your manhood

suicide is taking better care of others
than you do yourself.

Green Leaves

heading out

on that particular day
i carried through the day
fighting demons that my family
would never expect me to be fighting
the night before
i cried myself to sleep
in our hotel room
lying next to him as the dark of the night comforted me.
he fell asleep, half listening as i told him my testimony
unbothered, unaware, and uninterested
and for the longest i was not able to move on
as i watched him hold on and let go of me at the same time

day 0

i-75
it was not premeditated –
it was my subconscious
all of those thoughts surfaced to the front.
he said i kept grabbing the steering wheel
threatening to kill us both
i do not remember
i only recall being high off of emotions
i saw the empty space in my mother's eyes
when she reached the top of the hill
to greet me so we could go home
i saw nothing but rage
i stood by as the paramedics tried to restrain me
Angela
i remember her voice
as she was praying in the background
i do not know what happened exactly
i just needed prayers that day

i lost it
completely
watching the winds tease the trees as if the joke was all on
me
eight years later, on the side of the highway
i found myself hallucinating.
terribly bad

look! a green leaf

i am still unsure of how i got from the hospital to the psych
ward
how did they think i would get the help i needed in here?
the next few days consisted of solitary confinement
me losing my sanity
eyes twitching
wrist slitting
and family visits
new medications
new friends
new experiences and new diagnoses
where is my mother?
where is my baby?
what happened to my degree?
did i graduate college?
i do not remember
the asylum swallowed me whole and spit me out after 17
days

day 1

i woke up this morning and went out of my room
i saw jesus there
standing with the doctors and counselors
i walked over to his wheelchair to inform him
that i am not taking any more medication
and i want to be released from here
jesus ignored me
white coats surrounded me
my roommate next to me
repeatedly banged his head on the wall until it leaked blood
i want to go home
will i die here?

the one i blame

i was 15 when i first wanted to die
i heard my heartbeat through my ears
each night i tried lying on my stomach
but it just didn't feel right
me, hiding from the world when
i missed my period 9 years ago

my life became one big run on sentence ever since

iwishiwastakingmylastbreathandnotyou

the moment after i took the pregnancy test
i knew that i would be doomed
this was the second worst day of life for me

—————

it's so hard for me to try and find the right words to say
i'm so sorry we never got the chance to meet
i have an image of you
in my mind
an image
something i'll never let go of
i'll do nothing but wish you were here

———

just one mistake

your fetus defeated me.
a boy or girl, i'll never know.
the love i had for you?
i will never be able to show
but i wrote this to show you that i care.
this pain,
the hurt,
at times
i cannot bear.

i wonder what life would be like if i kept you.
it was a such a tough decision to make at 15 years old

bloody nikes on the odd little table

"do it."
it's your choice.
"just do it."
no, it's your choice.
"you will never think about it again."
but it's still your choice.
"i did it…"
yea, i'm just telling you. but it's your choice.
"you won't feel anything." but…the choice is yours.
"you're too young to raise a baby."
but you have to make up your mind.
"god will forgive you."
do it

day 2

the male nurse reminded me of him
i walked over and slapped the nurse in the face
and that is when revenge came
as he spit in my face
threw me in a room and slammed my toe in the door
resulting in my toenail ripping
it took six cops to restrain me today
i just want to go home

parenthood unplanned

seeing you through that screen beating for your life hurt me
to my core
you opened your heart to me and now my heart pumps with
regret
words will never define the darkness
of how letting you go was the biggest mistake of my life
and if this is what they meant by you learn from your
mistakes then i have a triple PhD.
i'll never learn from this.
i love you
i could apologize for the vicious attack you endured
because of me
but it won't make it right.
you deserved more than what you would have received
from me at that moment in my life

just do it

i cannot forget the pieces of you that fell off of my body.
how do you deal with your child being stranded when you
caused the eviction?

i didn't know that when you died, i would too.
how could something so painful be so recommended?

day 3

those idiots
i woke up to all of those
insane people
until i took a look around and realized that i was a crazy
person too

HELP

fifteen is too young to bare

i'm a sorry mama
i'm young and I don't know how to be a mama
i'm sorry mama
sorry mama
God will never give you the chance to conceive again
you sorry mama
how could you mama?
are you a mama?
a selfish mama
not you, mama.
"ma'am?"
okay
i'll do it mama.

day 4

don't you people know that i need sunlight?
the cuts on my skin

the bruises on my legs
i am tired of being strapped in a strange bed
they make me wear strange clothes
i do not want to go to today's focus group
no matter how much medication they give me
there is no pill to make my demons go away

———

you were eleven the day your first love
forced your thighs open
you were fifteen the day your doctor
spread your legs to remove the seed
even though you were the product of my brokenness,
you will always be the product of everything i ever
dreamed of.
today
would have been
your tenth birthday
today you would wake up with a smile just like mine
today
you would have many gifts to unravel
today
my family does not know it's your birthday
those who encouraged me to dispose of you
never speak of you anymore
to them
you are old news

no one was there to hold my hand during the abortion
whore
baby killer
these are all words that greeted me as the bystanders held
their posters
they were right.

abortion is not an easy fix
it is destroying

—

could you raise a child to be your favorite mistake?
will you have an answer when my son asks where his father
is?
i raped my baby of his voice
this is why i choose to speak.
they say it's not too late for an abortion
but it's not too late to keep your baby either
don't be so quick to get rid of your evidence

—

i became the punchline to bad abortion jokes
blood rests on my hands
my body is not up for debate anymore
i am no longer a supreme-court case
i am a permanent decision
to temporary fear
encouraged
pressured
i am so sorry this was even a choice
screw those who make a living off of death
and later go home to their families
while politicians applaud
this lame excuse for a
woman's choice

abortion is not freedom

i have lived in a prison of pain for the past 10 years
i felt the need to hide the life inside of me to be accepted
i am sorry i felt that my life would end
if i did not end yours
that if i did not go through with it
i would not get an education
but
if the baby was really the problem then why do i still feel
like dying inside?
what happens when churches give cold stares as you walk
through the congregation fifteen and pregnant?

———

i think he was a he
and i think he would have looked exactly like me
i would have told him stories about his grandfather
how he left when i was one
i would have taught him everything that my mother taught
me
i would tell him
all of the things that happened before he was born

———

day 5

where is my child?
where is my pastor?
where is my best friend?
where is jesus?
here comes another tray of food

bloody nikes hurt my feet

i lost my dignity
i lost my fearlessness
trying to live with the weight of death on my shoulders
i felt disgusting in a world full of living things
being smothered by the painful reminders
that i am a murderer
it is dark now
i cannot get the sun back
yet
no one saw the darkness surrounding me
and i've been praying for the ceasefire of my spirit ever
since
i cannot breathe through these lungs anymore
a piece of my soul was removed
how am i still here?

it is hard to say that i am alive
when there is an empty space where my baby used to live
you are supposed to be here with me
yet
i let my miracle slip through the cracks of my portal of
consent

i allowed my womb to become a tomb
i still let the tears you would have cried

come alive in my eyes
abortion is not freedom
abortion is not love
and
every time it rains
i picture you crying from the sky
i was impregnated with broken dreams
and yes
i still had the milk around my mouth
but being 'just a baby' does not give you the right to abort
your own
the doctor told me that your heartbeat could not be heard
you were too small
the size of a thumb
and it was okay to proceed with the murder

choice

is it really?
a choice is not given to the one whose life is taken away
a holocaust
a murder
yes
words that are not easy to hear
but need to be heard
and
i will not opt for a softer word

day 6

i woke up to my doctor's face holding pills that i refused to
swallow
those people strapped my arms so tightly against the
hospital bed because

they said i tried to harm myself
i became a danger to myself when
i just wanted peace within
i got tired of hiding the truth
hiding me
i lost it
literally
every problem i tried to deal with turned into a bigger
problem
thinking i could escape the world
when i knew my pain would never fade
hiding the truth
hiding me
running from my pain
i thought i escaped
i was scared to face the pain
and so i kept running

if all babies go to heaven then all hitmen must go to hell.

wings of forgiveness

when i think of my seed
i imagine you looking so much like me.
i imagine you being smart, beautiful, and talented
i am the mother of a dead baby
a murderer
i made a legal yet god awful decision
i was fifteen
i remember being the youngest one there
the lobby was full
and you would think they were giving out free food
vouchers like
'aye, let me get an abortion with extra sauce.'

the clinic was packed.
i met a lady who became my friend for one day only
she had 7 kids and could not afford 8
i wish that i could go back.
i looked around for my mother
i cried the whole way there and home
gloomy, but
'once it wears off, she'll be fine.'
said the doctor
i wasn't
i'm still not,
probably never will be
but,
it happened.

birth ctrl+ alt+delete the fetus.

one last hit

the hitman collected his blood money and disposed of my
dead baby
its dead flesh remains inside of me
i threw up all the way home
i bled for days after and
people said things but had no way of fixing me
the moment i got up from that table
he took my baby's blood and bones
but he never disposed of his spirit
i never healed from that abortion.

a walking coffin

at night i feel the shadows of your tiny fingers creeping on
my neck
holding on for dear life
and when i sit still
i hear your cries
you ask
mommy what is that big silver clamp thing nearing my
head?

when seeds speak

mommy
wouldn't you want to see me play?
i know there is another option for me
i've been counting the days until we meet
mommy, each day is getting shorter
mommy? remember, whatever decision you make cannot
be undone
do you understand that mommy?

hello?
mommy
i can hear your thoughts and i feel your pain too
mommy
please give me a chance to live
don't listen to them mommy
don't just do it
i'm your seed.
please,
grab your shoes
and get the hell up off that odd little table.

day 7

Alice walks around giving false hugs
Ashley was there, screaming in empty space
my lights go dim as bedtime is near
trays are collected
coloring sheets become trash
and they walk me back to my room and pierce me to my
bed again
quiet
dark
and alone
i am not proud
who am i?
why am i here wasting away?
jesus roamed the halls in his wheelchair
claiming that he could save us all
in a psych ward trying to get better

day 8

i wrote a love letter to jesus explaining that we have to
break up
'it's not you, it's me'
i cannot pretend to know you
you are not who my grandmother says you are
and you are not where she said you would be
i need you here
at this very moment
no
i am not safe here
from the nurse who just spit in my face
and the nurse who twisted my nipples so hard, violating me
and hammering me to my room
i am in a foreign place
i want out
now
apart from these extremes
hardly can i believe this is part of your plan to save me
if this is heavens gates then i am leaving my key at the
leasing office
i want out
you are abusive
thank you

letter to Angela from greenleaf

dear Angela
thank you for your silent acceptance of the fact that
life is a pain sometimes too great to handle
you saw me clinging to hope
holding onto these hospital sheets
scared
frustrated and tired

i asked jesus to fix me and when i called
he sent me to voicemail
but you called me right back
you are a great secretary
taking all of my messages and leaving them on his bulletin
board for review
thank you for giving me supportive advice on how mental
illness does not define me
though my mouth and my brain are not on the same track
you were patient with me always
and for 10 years i have watched you pray for me
you taught me how to be alive
gazing on your knees at 3 am
thank you for encouraging me to keep the life i did not
want

straitjacket

at times i believe we writers are insane
all of us
there are those who revel in our trauma identities
as we are forced to put ourselves in shoes that we will
never be able to walk comfortably in
i wrote diligently to try and release the demons boiling
through my veins
i wrote this book with the pink pen from the psych ward
my writer demons were driving me to madness
day by day
my pain scratched paper
i woke up in the bed of the in-patient psych ward
screaming to the top of my lungs
'calm down' they said
we will fix you and then you can go home
and then they carried me to the tub to wash away the blood
from the night before

day 9

my mind must have snapped from the strain
i now remember the ambulance driving up on i-75 to rescue
me
my heart oozed out a tired smile to the paramedics
i am not worth saving
please put me down

that green leaf turned black fast
the moment i collided with my internal demons
group sessions and lunch trays
17 long days
solitary confinement
tell me where the time went?

day 10

love should never cost you your sanity
i hate the environment that i am in
i no longer like what i see
who is to blame for my insecurities?
i walk with my head down
i stay awake at night
i cannot sleep,
i am filled with so much negativity until negativity became
me
but i lie and carry on smiling because it does not make
anyone question
self-hate consumes me
i was too busy loving everyone else and forgot how to love
me
i terrorize myself as i try to pick myself up again
i resort to late night cries
i wonder why i hate myself

day 11

i am not doing great
i think i am going through depression and anxiety
suicidal thoughts
i hate my depressive episodes
i just eat more and sleep less
locked in this room
away from the world
my self-confidence is gone
i feel like i cannot get anything done
i just think i am not good enough
i feel so weak
i feel really low
if you're reading this
are you okay?

——

i toss and turn in a bed of discomfort
between the walls of pro choice
and pro-life
society please shut up.
abortion is not a wonderful procedure
full of sunflowers and rainbows
with pots of gold at the end
and you know that
signed,

the
slut
whore
baby murderer

under the influence

i reminisce on how they gave me a white pill to put me to
sleep
and how i wanted to get my things and storm out of the
clinic
but the pill was much stronger than i was at the time
and it was only then that they gathered me
took me to the back
and disposed of my dead baby

mommy murder

my heart still thumps loudly at the sight of other chocolate
babies
my baby
you remind me so much of me
and at night i hear you crying
i can feel you tugging at my breasts.
gravity
working against me as universal laws of attraction work
collectively to keep me down
i weep in peace
because if dragging me down to the pits of hell is where i
belong
i will kindly rest
i will burn twice as much
for you

conceiving you was a promise that i should have kept
and if the choice was really mine
you'd still be here but
i was sunken into the pressure of hanging myself with my
own womanhood
people expected me not to feel hurt but
i'm still a mother to a dead baby
i was a child who decided not to have a child
caged in the center of pro-choice and pro-life
and some view me as a woman who is not wrong in the
choice i made
some say i took control over my pregnancy
but how much control do you have at 15?
i'm a murderer
it should have been my last breath and not my baby's

———

the forbidden grief
hurt me mentally
as i went in with a baby and walked out empty
i consider the abortion as a failure in my life
something i never want to relive

i have intervened with many women
who ask me if they should just do it
i saved someone else's baby on occasions i care not to
mention
even when i did not have the strength
and courage to save my own

abortions are done out of fear
fear of society
fear of failure
false
evidence
appearing
real
the hurt associated is not explainable
there is no secular answer for it
i was in shock
painful
i could not believe myself
and
i ate
to numb the pain
i had nightmares of babies
i started hiding my pain
i could not deal with suffering
and
self-destructive tendencies
irritability
anxiety
fear of god's punishment

flashbacks
sexual dysfunction
lack of bonding with small children
psychological numbness
anger or rage
repression
denial of feelings
overprotection
unresolved guilt
depression
nightmares

———

there was a soul living inside of me
when i woke up from the operating bed
the feeling that i felt was indescribable
i realized too late that this was the wrong decision
but there was no turning back from the anesthesia
we part only to meet again

———

table of regret

i meditated and i wrote to my baby
to explain why i did what i did
i learned to attempt to forgive myself
and
forgive my partner
i was not thinking for myself
i felt worst after i left
oh
how i entered the hospital with a life and left with death

the nurse's card

i hate seeing you cry
i hate how much it hurts you every single time
i wish i can take the pain away and make you see what i see
i hate watching you beat yourself up all the time
you are destroying yourself from the inside
when you are perfectly fine
you are a beautiful walking sunshine in my eyes
being you is enough
no, you don't have the perfect body
but please do not tear yourself apart like this
i watch you struggling to cope every day and i just want to
be able to help

day 12

constant frustration to fill this void
smoking makes me feel whole
a big part of me, it became
the missing key
it completed me

no matter how hard i try to be okay
i am not
and it sucks
i know people tell me to love myself
but it's not as simple as that
not when you feel so numb
my childhood was dark
i felt angry most of the time
a feeling that was always there
hard to explain
here i am
wishing it would all go away
i wish things were different
observing other people's life
as happiness seems to come to them so naturally
and yes, i know it can be misleading but
when you feel so empty
you so desperately want that.
love and happiness
do i sound crazy?
craving happiness makes me feel like something is so
wrong with me
but if you ask me
i'll say that i'm fine

day 13

i lost myself during the process
even if i take pills for that
depression will always be in my head
no one talks about how painful it is to let go of someone
who
is not deserving of you
i want to continue to pour myself into him in hopes
that someday he will see my worth

i feel drained and i question everything about myself

i do not want to show this part of me to the outside world
i think so low about myself
i am in a vicious cycle that rarely ends the way i want it to

———

i hated myself after being asked by people
i did not think i deserved to live
why did i deserve to live but my baby did not have a
choice?

———

i believe that God knows i was
not strong enough to deal with everything i was going
through

———

day 14

in order to change how i feel i have to look within
all of those thoughts and feelings i try so desperately to
hide
open my mind
become free
for the first time in a long time
today
i'm going to let myself breathe
today i choose me

day 15

since you've been here,
you reduced yourself to ugly
and your self-hate has filtered itself into every inch of your
body
i hate seeing you so incredibly unhappy
i hope one day you realize that you have more to offer to
the world
more importantly, right now in this moment
i want you to know just how incredibly perfect you are
to me
life does not care about what you have and don't have
it cares not about your stress levels
or if you cried yourself to sleep the night before
please keep going
from me to me

mute

i still struggle to heal from abortion
remember whatever decision you make cannot be undone
to some, i represent freedom and pro-choice
my lips are lined with shame
no one feels my pain
where pro-choice and pro-life meet
most of the time i walk around silent and defeated

seems like i almost loved the abuse
settling for mistreatment is an indication of how
you feel about yourself
the world values you the way you value yourself

————

unmute

the moment i started speaking up for myself is when i lost
all of my friends
i have learned that people are comfortable with you as long
as you do not
speak

mo·les·ta·tion

noun

1. sexual assault or abuse of a person, especially a woman
or child
2. it means to lay next to a child and start toying with her
body
3. to touch her in places that you would not want anyone to
touch your child
4. it's when little girls look up to you for guidance and you
lead them to deception
6. it's your hands and how they found their way to undoing
the zipper on my pants as you guide me to allow you to
discover what lies beneath
7. it's how the smile on my face does not really show how i
feel and my eyes could not allow you to see my depth as
you continue to insert yourself inside of me

good christian girls are supposed to shut their mouths

i am no longer an object to your will
doing what you say
believing what you believe
being your puppet

my body belongs to me
yet
for so long i had no say
i was maneuvered by you
somehow you dictated my body
as a child
and you dictated my mind as i grew older
sexually mistreating me
emotionally mistreating me
mentally mistreating me

it's enough of being silent

———

many nights
i tried washing
you off of me
my skin
my hair
my nails
my memories
the blur
everything failed
and failed
again
surrounded by people
who blamed me for my rape

seventeen
drunk
hotel room
mad dogs
fake friends
random guys
all my fault
i brought this on myself

did he rape my head too?

———

a coma would be nice

though i was in the comfort
of friends
'fri'
'ends'
where my freedom ends
as cheap
becomes
expensive
at my fountains end
as i slept
for what dreamt like forever

anonymous blog question

"my friend was at our party and she got really drunk and
had sex with this guy. she claims she cannot really
remember what happened, but she's been acting distant,
weird, and withdrawn from us since then. was she raped?"

response

was she wobbling?
yes
was she too drunk to fully consent?
yes

when someone doesn't consent
that's sexual assault
he should not have had sex with your friend
if she was that drunk
support her
tell her that it's not her fault
thank you for supporting her
as her boundaries were crossed

god is a strong black woman

and so many people bad mouthed me,
but i remained silent.
even down to family—
people came to me saying she said this or
he said that
and i stayed silent
i continued to smile when i saw them in person.
i used my mouth to bless anyone that cursed me
i forgave family
forgave friends for stabbing me
and kept my distance
walking side by side
with God
in silence
she always defended me
protected me
promoted me
she blessed me
built me up in their presence and now they are silent
and regret putting their mouths on me
when those tables turned

day 16

my straitjacket came loose
i am being moved to building a
with the less crazy people
i have been on good behavior
i will have new roommates
new bed sheets
and i can finally wear regular clothes.
i can walk freely
and i can rejoice
i have phone privileges
i can call mom and dad
i will be on my best behavior tonight

machine

at a young age
men started ripping me open to see what was inside
i grew accustomed to my body being treated like a machine
something built of metal
that can be used relentlessly,
deconstructed and easy to assemble
though they never cleaned my parts
and put me back together.

most left me to rust
they would leave after my love meter raised
they dis-assembled me like the scrap metal collected by my
father
praying that their mothers and daughters do not end up like
me – scraps of metal

eight

i have an issue when men raise their voices
it troubles me
takes me back to being young
and hiding in my closet
praying for better days.

please communicate to me without screaming to
the top of your lungs

dad

my father's incarceration caused him to physically miss a
full decade of my life. i can vividly remember going to visit
him in prison and how the jailers didn't allow me to sit in
his lap. i became detached from male love after being
ripped away from the first man i ever loved.
oh, how that was the most heartbreaking thing ever
being ripped away from my own father's lap as a child,
because it was against prison policy.
i can literally feel the pain of my ancestors being sold and
separated from their parents
how the jailers ripped me away from daddy's lap
and made me hush all at once.
don't cry baby,
don't cry.

daddy issues blues

there were times i hated my father for
being away
not understanding the concept of prison
as my vagina became one big jail cell
at 11 years old
trying to fill an empty void of love
that should have been given to me
from my biological father
not daddy
but father
teach me how a man should love a woman
emotionally
because truth be told
sex satisfies emotions and
that's it.
thus,
sex for me helped me
when i felt empty

i released the need to blame my father for my relationship
with men

day 17

i did not come this far to only come this far
i am up again
i cannot be stopped
the adversaries tried everything
yet nothing could keep me down
the morning after i realized i did not truly kill myself

i took a look in the mirror and said thank you
to myself
i made it another day and
once more, i pulled myself out of hell

Welcome Home

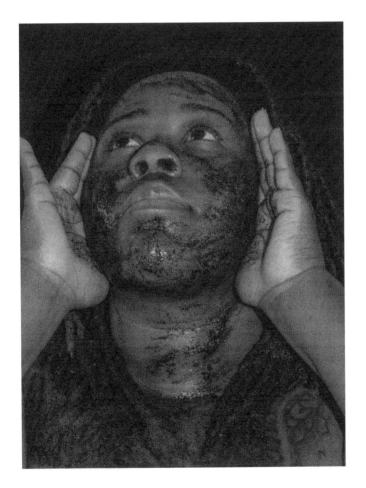

maybe
to get found
you have to get lost along the way

going sane

spending days in a psych ward teaches you a lot about
people
i learned that all suffering is valid and that it is okay
because
pain rarely follows the rules
i never learned her name
but she gave me advice that i still hold closely to me
on those days when i wanted to fall asleep and never wake
up

i learned to give my darkness a voice of reason because if i
continue to shut it up,
internal demons will take control and speak for me.

the insane asylum became my home until i learned how to
be myself again
when i was released my family had all welcomed me
my mom told me that he checked on me every day
she gave me my cell-phone back and he was the first
person i called
"hello—
i am so glad you're home
i love you and i miss you
i am afraid to leave my girlfriend for you because if i do
she may try to kill herself. you are so much stronger than
she is"

i do not think i am going to ever be enough for you
i stayed in my mother's backroom for days
i was afraid of the world and everyone knowing my secret
the more i remained locked in my room
the more harmful i became to my subconscious thoughts

home

every night my bed reminded me of a psych ward
i was so afraid of going back to that place
i came home and tried to wash 2009 out of my hair
thoughts of ending my life were still constant
and attempts were not far off
i could not stand myself
if i could stay in my room for 365 days
i would have
"you need to dress up" i can't.
"please cut your hair." i won't
"start over" i will
"what happened to you? you fell off!"
i did

depression will swallow you whole
like quicksand
and it won't always spit you out.
learn to crawl until your knees bleed
you have your ancestor's blood and will-power
inside of you

free yourself

————

for attention

i will never forget the day that
my enemy showed up as my friend
belittling me behind my back
blatantly telling the world that
i was having episodes for attention
that truly hurt

who gets attention out of being mentally sick?
i am left to wonder how much attention i would have gotten
if i would have let depression kill me
i was so close to dying
she would have been the first one at my funeral
bending over at my casket
for attention

get out of my room.

never allow love to make you desperate.

i will never understand why the depths of my worth
was so deeply embedded in another human being.
at times i am embarrassed by the things that i used to accept
but when i tell you about my past
it's not for you to feel sorry for me
but for you to understand who i am
where i have been
and where i am going

―――

most of my relationships were one sided
feed me
sex me
entertain me, emotionally and sexually
i lost myself trying to find men

———

frontstabbing

i overlooked
my scars because i was in love with the person holding the
knife
narcissistic abuse was a part of my journey
but it will not be my final destination

forgive yourself for tolerating them as long as you did
always look a man in his eye and you will see his truths

circle

i almost gave in and you almost caught me slipping
you almost had me.
you almost killed me and i almost let you.
again.
22 years of not knowing my worth seem to be trying to
overpower the 1 year that i have discovered it
here i am
after rehab
traveling down i75
doing 80 in a 60
anxious to see you
addicted to the pain

i do not love him
i loved his brokenness
i fed off of it and became obsessed with his flaws
brokenness drips through him
he was broken when i met him
i did not ruin him
i was so flawed to think that if he drinks from my fountain,
all of his troubles would be washed away

can you see how toxic i was?

—

the problem wasn't me belonging to you
it was that you never did belong to me

you never noticed me crying myself to sleep
your shoulders of love were built for me to cry on
you kissed my nightmares away
lying in the dark as the night comforted me
unbothered, unaware, and uninterested in wiping my tears
i carried through most days fighting demons
that you would never expect me to fight alone
tears were my only solace
and though my face may be smiling by morning,
by nightfall the mask will come out

———

what does real love feel like?

real love is not draining

the truth is i was dead before you met me
i looked for you to bring me back to life
to remove the knife
from my back
i was drafted so far away from myself and have been trying
to find my way back ever since
i literally tried to bury myself alive
i was harmful to myself
degrading myself into nothingness
i had so much more to live for
always hungry for more

men will stay because they feel sorry for you

i could be anything in the world but i wanted to be his.
it's not what we left undone that hurts
it's what we could have built
that is what stings

the one that got away

the way your mother jokes about her son being 'just like his
daddy'
is perplexing.
i always miss the joke.
could she see things in you that i could not?
or could she see herself in me?

kept

i wanted to pull the trigger
thank you God for a praying grandmother

may

i still remember how you left me in the car
with blood in my eyes
you watched me cry
wiped my face with your rough hands
and cut me deeper

may

graduation day
i walked across the stage
with my heart dragging the floor
knowing that you were in the crowds
rooting
but not for me
you were rooting for the
root to your tree

from a "piece of a man is better than no man at all"

i reduced my worth for men
telling myself i would rather be the woman he cheats with
than the woman he cheats on

narcissistic texts

i was broken and you said i should be over it by now
get over it— you said repeatedly
why does it still make you cry?
haven't you moved on?

i wasted a lot of time with men since the very beginning
i allowed my desire to be loved to lead me to desperation
i have learned to wait for eligible men.

clean hands

you are not a bad person
we simply had a bad experience
created by both of our
dirty
hands
overtime
i am fully responsible for the parts
that i played
i see myself in you in a lot of ways
but
as i forgive you
i am forgiving myself
as i release you
i release old parts of me
and i want you to
be
free
and
promise to never
live through another
bad experience
but
create love
peace
and happiness overtime
your love drove me to look into the mirror and question my
reflection
overall, you taught me how to overcome my weakest self

thank you

———

wilted garden

i thought that i could not stand to see you with anyone else
but me
but now i know the meaning behind god will break your
heart to save your soul
i know what it's like to be broken
to feel worthless
hopeless
but at the end of that despair lies happiness
peace
you dig
and you dig
until you find that reason to live
you forgive yourself
you apologize to yourself
and you learn to accept your past mistakes
you keep growing
watering
nourishing yourself
no negative self-talk
only
prosperity and growth

_____

old dixie highway

i am not a one-night stand
i am marriage and lifelong partnership
i am not a snack
i am full course
a meal
waiting to be devoured
by the heart that is meant to love me

note to self:

just because you expected a different outcome for your
relationship doesn't mean you're not getting the
relationship you actually asked for
this is what happens when we settle
you will continue to attract the same partner until you
decide to attend to emotional wounds

bad relationships can trigger unhealed trauma
but
remaining broken is a choice

———

love is not blind
you showed me exactly who you were
but i chose to ignore the patterns thinking i could have the
power to change you
but you changed me instead
love changed me
love opened my eyes
love is sometimes naive instead of blind

i will not wait at the end of the promise you made me

when heartbreak feels like drinking acid

i met a lady who sat next to me in the lobby waiting for the
therapist
she smiled and made loud outbursts to herself frequently
i clenched my mother's thigh as i was afraid to be
surrounded by people who were mentally ill
until i realized i was much like those people
the lady caught me staring
as i scooted closer to mom

mom started telling me that she knew her from high school
before the incident
someone poured acid in her drink
she became my equal
out of her mind
she walked over to me and waved

she uttered my mother's name as if she remembered her
'they poured acid in my drink one night at the club'
she said

we were one in the same
sitting
waiting
hoping
the therapist could make us better that day

therapists can't fix me either

two days later,
my therapist resigned.
he turned in his license from practicing.
was i broken to the point of no repair?

temporary home

between my legs was the warmest place you knew
why did you become so cold after i let you in?

my true feelings had to be squeezed to make room for
yours
but
thank you for indirectly teaching me what not to look for in
a husband
i discovered what not to stand for as a woman
and as the daughter of a king
thank you for not always being truthful to me
your actions were inconsistent but i let my heart love you
anyway
your deception helped me to differentiate between a king
and a clown with a crown
it is not good to fall in love with words
and i learned that songs do not make up for past mistakes

i do not regret our moments because you taught me things
about me

without deception
i would not know how to appreciate truth. thank you for
teaching me how to forgive those who wronged me
i learned a lot through watching us fail.
it is not your fault that i was broken.
you could not fix yourself, so how could i expect you to fix
me?
my desire was to fix you yet i had no idea of how to fix me

——

you saw me as a broken woman,
concluding that broken is all that i would ever be
not understanding that i was not broken,
i was simply being shaped into divine purpose.

———

my entire worth was once misplaced into the hands of being good enough for someone else instead of being enough for myself.

———

i had trouble getting rid of my demons because i enjoyed their company. i became a host for them until i almost let them burn my entire house down.

———

iPhone notepad secrets

tonight
i got a hotel room
and you came
to make me cum
and yet i still felt empty
why continue to get high if you're living low?

men only do what we allow

i became nothing with you even though i still wanted to
stay.

at the time i loved deeply
desperately wanting to be loved back
though i realized that if i ever experienced love
during that state of mind
i would not have known what to do with it

——

old new beginnings

what life means without you
i do not want to witness
you are like sugarcane in the summertime
sweet in all the right places
even though some parts of you are bitter,
i still crave you
my heart knows when you are near
beating for you to come closer
and undress me
you speak to my soul
you understand all that it needs to feel whole
you know all of my secrets
and you kiss away my insecurities

when i can't go on
you keep me going
you keep my river flowing
and i love you for that
please
don't ever let the well run dry

depression is a verb
used to describe one who
puts on their best
outfit to protect insecurities

———

the doctor was wrong about my diagnosis
i was not depressed
i was surrounded by negative energy
negative things
negative people
i replaced those negatives with positives
replaced heartbreak with lessons learned
and depression
soon vanished for me

from me to me

maybe you should stop eating your pain and address it
you have created a body and dumped toxic emotions into it

free yourself

if one more person tells me that i'm pretty for a big girl, i
just might lose it.
i'm pretty all around
what does my size have to do with anything?

———

though i always struggled with weight issues,
my emotional eating disorder became full-blown after the
abortion
getting in touch with such feelings is fundamental to
recovery.
the resistance, denial, and fear of abortion is a threatening
topic for most women
i could not speak about it until i stopped angrily blaming
others.
a lot of unexplored and unresolved feelings were being
exposed
through my relationships

———

garden tool

stop yourself before you begin to grow flowers in his
garden
do not cultivate his veins, his heart, and his head
to think only perfect thoughts
do not sit by his bed of flowers any longer to make sure he
gets the perfect amount of sun and water
love, soil and proper nourishment
that man is not a garden that you can nourish to a better life
you are not his help
you may be ruining him
you just want to fix him and that is not love
he is not your project to keep you busy
you only keep him so you can make him perfect.
that's not love
you are too toxic for him
ruining him and making him think
that since brokenness sprouts,
he needs help.
but you cannot help him
you cannot make him hate himself for wilting you
tend to your own garden work

dehydration

water only the people who water you

you are not a place-holder while he gets his shit together

———

i served an eviction notice to the woman who once settled

do not dim your light
to love anyone who does not know how to love you
properly
do not feel ugly because the men who had you could not
appreciate your worth

———

your inability to love me reflected my inability to love
myself

Healing

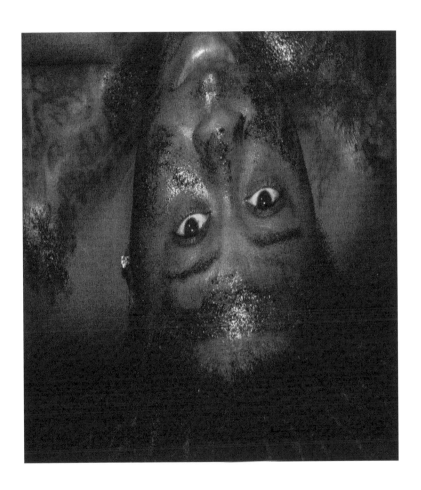

before i create a habit out of putting others before i put
myself,
i will remove myself entirely
i will do the necessary work to heal myself
i deserve the best of everything
and my supporters deserve the best version of me

———

heal yourself first. the rest will come later.

i am not my sister's keeper: i am my sister.
May God use me to heal her.

shifting generations

because I kept going,
so will other women.
because i choose to heal
over hurting,
so will other women.
because i found the beauty
in my brokenness,
so will other women

when i first started writing it became a private hobby
writing became my limb
the church was somewhat my safe haven
i stood firm telling my testimony
but i still felt constipated
in fact i felt worse

pastors prophesied while church members judged
seems like every problem i tried to deal with
turned into a bigger problem
and my pastor became a babysitter who was always on the
phone

as i began to heal
my spirit of discernment began picking men apart
i could see right through the false images of who men were
selling themselves to be
and i finally opened my eyes to see the true colors of
vultures

responsibility

never blame anyone for your pain
do not give them that power because
it is not their right
and when you blame them for your pain
you then hire them for your healing
when in actuality
your healing is your responsibility

i am great.
i am a journey.
i am a sky.
i am free.
don't try to put ceilings on my skies.
my mind wanders deeper than you could ever
swim

i am isolated.
i am restored
i am smiling again
i am happy
i am peace

i am going to live out my purpose
i will become who i have always wanted to be
not living under constraint
by shackles of my past.
i did not come this far to only come this far.
i came this far to only go further.
i am proud of overcoming
i am never satisfied
i will always push for me
more growth, more greatness
if love's journey was not challenging, my final destination
would be pointless

i am learning to accept my past
and to be honest about the pain that lies in my DNA
the same pain has become the building blocks
of my mitochondria

pain comes with healing
no matter how bro-ken
i appear to be
i realize i am never too broken to put myself back together
again

you are who you've been waiting for
the apology is never coming and it
does not mean that you don't deserve it but it's simply not
coming
release the need for closure and
forgive yourself

———

progression over pain

my past has been great practice
underneath the beauty i now live in,
lies a ton of self-healing that i had to do.
the beginning of healing had a lot to do with me
looking my pain in the face
facing hurt head on.
my insecurities kept me constipated
but i surrendered the brokenness.

for me, it is not about the product
it is about the process
because life hits hard but can you keep going?
you have to

racing to the altar

rather than forcing men to marry you or see your worth,
you should appreciate the fact that he does not want to rush
because healing can't be rushed. and if you do not heal
first, you will bruise him
be gentle
your healing is your responsibility
his healing is his responsibility
it is not a mans job to clean you up and
its not your job to clean him up
he has to do his work and you have to do your work

show up for yourself

one of the greatest challenges was knowing when to let go
and when to fight harder

be willing to work on your negatives.
it is okay to explain to a man that you think he is great
but right now
you are too toxic to be in a healthy relationship

take yourself off the dating market and clean up your heart

———

i soon realized that i was actually breaking up with a
wound and not a person
though he was the vessel god chose to use
as the segway to my healing
so that i could finally unpack my emotional baggage
every season serves its purpose

i lost you but i found me

_____

keep breathing
keep living
keep laughing

do not allow your hurt to delay your healing

———

servant

you would be amazed at the things a desperate
woman would do to keep a man
i became
disgusted
and surprised at my efforts

a woman will forget who she is
and become a servant.
but a wise woman will bounce back

being the wise wombman that i am
i learned to be no ones servant
but to only serve my best and highest self.
the love i thought i needed externally
was buried deeply within
misplaced at a young age
but i deliberately sent my older self to grab the young me
by the hand
and walk through life together to remove pain
layer, by layer
and now, i heal.
i bleed
i heal some more.
i nourish myself
i clean my wounds not bury the wounds
i am falling in love with myself all over again

i stopped looking for what i thought i could find in men
and i found it in mc

heal others as you heal yourself
no one can love you the way you need to love you

———

being speechless when my family asks about you makes me realize that a lot of things still hurt.

_____

i tolerate the pain
so stoic
"she's so strong,
so brave, so beautiful and powerful"
but they don't know
that i've been hurt more times than anyone could imagine
i grew accustomed to the pain
but
i wanted to
truly find myself

i was intentional about burning through my flesh
and bleeding
i turned myself inside out

it was the only way that i could move forward

———

as i heal myself,
i continue to heal the little girl inside of me.

———

give thanks for every time you self-healed after being broken.

_____

do not get so comfortable with pain that you do not make
space for healing

to do list after heartbreak:
heal
grow
help others
deal with the truth about yourself without getting
upset
evict your inner liar
love on yourself
be patient with yourself
refrain from trying to heal and date at the same time
eradicate negative self-talk
affirmations in the morning, noon, and night
understand that prayer is talking to god and
meditation is listening: use them both
do not explain your no
be the wise woman who builds her emotional home
and not the foolish woman that tears it down
don't waste your energy on things and people who
do not matter
forgive

additional tools to heal:

shea butter
sunlight
repeatedly kiss your wounds
loc your hair and remind yourself you're beautiful

unacknowledged emotions inside of you will eventually
rupture
allow your emotions to have a voice

address what needs to be addressed
and release the rest

———

allow yourself to feel what you are feeling
welcome pain and the feelings that you feel
because those feelings need attention too
make peace with your pain
make peace within and
when its time is up
show pain the door and slam it shut

———

what i learned from love

you either take the warning or you take the lesson.

i will not wish hurt on you
only healing
because hurting me shows me
that you need healing more than hurt

_____

my emotional suitcase is full
through speaking i unpack
opinions of others
negative-self talk
trauma
and i replace it with
self-love
forgiveness
healthy friendships
and speaking my truths

control what you can control (you) and let the rest go
(them)

———

no monkey business

i am a woman first
and i will not allow a man to swing in and out of my life

may god use all of your past pain to generate your future
power

shovel

self-love does not always come first
sometimes it is buried so deeply under the mask of our
emotions
but it is our duty to keep digging until we rediscover what
we lost

love me deeper

i am my longest relationship.
i must fully love me first,
heal and commit to me only
healing is everyday work and
all you own is yourself

sacred space

before i am anyone else's
i belong to me
i command my legs to open and close
my body belongs to me
i reclaim my time
my energy
my space
my words

i am a force to be reckoned
i am in control of my body
i have the final say
always

———

people will justify you not loving yourself as their frame
for not loving you.
teach people how to respect you
through respecting yourself

——

love yourself until your cup runneth over
loving you means accepting you
accepting your past
owning your bullshit
and freeing yourself

———

beware of emotional manipulation. do not become
psychologically and emotionally subjugated to anyone

refused brokenness

i do not want anyone to mold me nor repair past hurt
i am aware of the damage that has been done
love me where i am
for who i am
in this very moment

if you're going to cry over a guy
at least make sure he has extraordinary powers

when you don't or can't acknowledge your feelings or accept something about yourself, it's a sign that deep down, you don't love yourself and if you don't love yourself, you will never find peace with those around you. unless you learn to love yourself and accept yourself and your feelings, you will never be able to love or be loved by anyone else either

____

love all of you like you are magic and you will find
yourself being completely loved by others

———

new energy who dis

it is me or you
and i choose me, always

i will not thank you for hurting me
but i will thank you for the decisions you made toward me
thank you for being great practice

i learned a lot from my scars
please do not look for self-love in someone else
never neglect you

i am not my mother's mistake
i am not the product of my father's failures
i am not my ancestor's short comings
i am not my great- grandmother's vicious cycles
i am free to make my own mistakes and learn from those
before me
i am free to openly speak to them about similar experiences
i am free to create my own path
free to think
free to breathe and feel
i will break generational curses
i am not my ancestors' pattern
i do not deserve dysfunctional relationships
i am responsible for being my best self
i am not a generational curse
i am not another statistic
i am not a burden
the vision i have for my life is my own

i will not die with skeletons in my closet
i am able to visit the dark places of my life without walking
down the same road
i am allowed to invest in myself
i am allowed to start over as much as i need to
i am allowed to cry
i give myself permission to feel pain
it is okay to not always be okay
i give myself permission to ask for help
no one defines me but me
i am enlightened into the reality of who i am
i am in control of my own destiny
i will not settle

----

to the receiving end of this book:

to work on yourself is the best thing you could do.
accept that you are not perfect, but you are enough.
and then start working on everything that destroys you.
insecurities
ego
dark thoughts
and in the end, you will see that you will make peace with
yourself and that is the greatest feeling in the world.

do not play life commitment games
with men who think you are good enough to live with
but not good enough to wife

‾‾‾‾‾

do not become broken by the misleading of immature and
insensitive men
i was released into a society that ate women alive

i was not taught about the realities that i would face as a
young woman growing up on the westside of Atlanta
what you refuse to learn at home, you will regurgitate in the
streets

people will convince you that you're nothing if you listen
to them

love yourself first

_____

you are worthy of a love that you do not have to beg for.

forgive yourself for not knowing what you didn't know
before you learned it.

———

do not wait until you are someone's first choice
wait until you are someone's only choice

_____

broken love affairs do not stop a powerful woman because a powerful woman is always focused on something greater.

temporary situations cannot break a woman who knows where she is headed.

———

i want to know what loving myself feels like
i convinced myself no one would want to be with someone
like me
there i was doing the best i knew how
helping everyone i know
become better
while they stand around and watch me self-destruct

_____

love will replenish
love does not distract
the right one does not stand in your way of being the best
version of you

———

discovering love

i'm here to tell you a love story
but it isn't your average love story
it isn't boy meets girl, though
it's arguably a more important one
and i say this because it tells a story of how i began to love
myself
you see,
i lost count of the number of times i've been called pretty
for a big girl
or beautiful with a 'but' behind it
you're pretty but you would look better if you lost weight
it's painful being a punch line behind every fat joke
i've been on every diet
starved the life in me because someone called me tubby
there was a time when i would only eat alone
emotional eater on an emotional roller coaster
i was ashamed to eat around people
i wouldn't even raise my hand all the way because i was
ashamed of my jiggle
i eat emotionally and hide behind my problems
my body was an apology to society
i'm tired of being viewed as something that needs to be
fixed
i'm just a piece
a side
i've been a last resort
boys assume that i have to feed on their scraps
i realize that i have so much more to live for
stop taking myself for granted
raise my damn hand to the highest
love myself
love myself
love myself

i'm still learning how to love the parts of me that no one
can see

found

i held onto someone who did not hold onto me when i
should have been holding onto myself

that was my problem.

i stopped asking every guy who shows me attention this
question: "are you here to stay?"
my past taught me not to be too trusting
i learned that words can be used as tools to lure me and that
those same words will be used to destroy me in the end.
words hold power
as the men reassured me that they will stay
i have instead just learned to nod in agreement even when i
know deep inside there is doubt devouring my soul
i only hope that this time it will be different

to my future husband:

i want to tell you everything about me even if my voice
shakes
how hard will it be to love me?
before i love you
i will love myself greater
for i know that you will be worth the risk of being cut open
once more
i will take small steps on the path to love because i
understand the risk of falling too quickly
may you and i have an incredibly deep relationship that
with time, will begin to soften your entry to my heart
and it will open wider, until i grant you access to
step through
yes
my voice will tremble and i may shatter but be prepared to
wipe my tears
i will be a love machine that works for nobody but you
it is my hope that you will find beauty behind all the scars
of my heart
and i will send secret messages to myself repeatedly: "give
love another try" until my mind becomes more accepting of
you
i never want to hear you say "i love that broken woman"
because i desire not to be placed in a narrative alongside
negative and untimely adjectives
i am a woman who has the power to love you like no other.
i am worthy of commitment and longevity
tell the world you love a woman who refused to be fixed
because honestly, she was never broken but –
simply mishandled in her past
i know how painful it is to be lied to
love me still
adore me still
have faith in me still

pray with me
laugh with me
clap for me
cry with me
please see things in my light and let me see things in yours
be content with me
be proud of me and support me as if i was the
manifestations waiting at the end of your prayer
i am just as worthy as everyone else
maybe you are the only one missing to make me whole
again. and maybe
i'll be the love you've constantly prayed for

if only you can stand to love a woman like me

fall in love with yourself
never expect to find your self-love
in someone else
the love you are trying to give others is the love you
deserve
you owe yourself the love that you keep trying to give

____

dysfunction is not love

i learned that insanity is when you love someone more than you love yourself. it's when you help them destroy you while trying to save them. insanity is not putting yourself first. insanity is trying to pour from an empty vessel

_____

going through heartache was needed for me to realign with the purpose of my existence

i am more than any failed friendship or relationship

———

forgive the people who have wronged you

only a woman can determine what she will and will not
stand for
guard your heart to avoid brokenness
create boundaries and love yourself more than you love that
other person
if you can't love yourself
how can you truly love someone else?
do not deny yourself of what you are worth.
do not wait for any person to bounce you around nor deny
you
love yourself or nobody will

————

always remember that
you need you

note to self:

do not define yourself by your subconscious negative
history

parasites do not stop being parasites. learn to stop being a host.

until you realize that you are a queen
you will keep getting played by a joker.
make sure you know the difference between a king and a
joker.

———

be selfish with your time, energy, and money.
vibrate so highly that you begin to attract what you desire
and what you deserve.
you are worthy of commitment
the universe will send you your heart's desire.
hold on to your inner promise.
i love you.
the hurt you feel,
the pain that you don't show
you will fill.
you will peel the hurt away layer by layer, but you must
first tell yourself that you deserve more

———

soar

follow your dreams
be patient
pray
don't be complacent

be proud of you for evolving
do not shrink
yourself to make other people feel comfortable

dear self

please do not settle
timing is everything and there is a love waiting for you

i am not disposable or unimportant. i am worthy of love, time, patience and adoration self-hate will not wipe your slate of a body clean

experience

just because you have not met the right one yet does not
mean you should settle
to be able to love other people, you must be able to love
yourself, at any given moment.

i survived what i thought would break me
let go of him and save yourself

dear self

i will always be your biggest fan
continue to live your life from the inside out
you are beautiful and i love you
you are a determined woman and you will always conquer
avoid relationships that might divorce you from yourself
make your well-being your top priority
become fully invested in personal development
do not take your eyes off of your goal
remain happy in your current state
celebrate small victories

———

i choose to be patient with you today and every day
because i overstand that angels have to learn how to fly

———

you are whole even if your heart is broken.

if he loves you

he will not destroy you

in the process of fixing myself
i discovered who i always was
i released and relinquished self-love

———

forgive yourself in order to progress yourself

self-mastery

failures are lessons that you come to learn and master
but you don't determine the curriculum
instead
you withstand life and its series of tests
laid out for you to learn

running shoes

i find myself running away from love, thinking that if i run
and hide, it will not find me. but what's the point of
running away from what is destined?

let love flow
i refuse to be a disservice to my life again.

dear self

you are the person i look up to the most
i do not feel guilty for starting over and getting to know
you again

this has been one of the most humbling experiences of my
life

i have loved and been loved and it is all equally life
changing

_____

i am still coming to terms with my past

poof

it all went up in smoke and i felt lost and scared but i found
more of myself as a result;
i learned how to truly let go
i became softer
kinder
wiser
more capable
more humble

self-love does not always come first
or second
or ever
self-love is created
it's not something that everyone has the opportunity to be
born with

self-love is cultivated—yes
self-love is harvested from the depths of the soul.

love arrives when love is supposed to

i look back on past relationships
truly believing that each one had a purpose
and
i no longer desire to change the past
because
the experiences were quintessential to my growth

_____

do not deny yourself of what you are worth.

challenge the parts of you that keep waiting for a person who is not showing up for your highest good.

how much money is in your self-love bank?

no re-entry

i have the power to forgive and release hurt from the prison
of my emotions
but my forgiveness does not grant you access to me again

learn how to grow through what you go through
i finally learned how to put myself back together again

let love come to you.

we attract the most beautiful things in life when we begin
to accept who we are.
the darkness of my past does not define my future

———

if you haven't learned by now: if a person sucks at love,
they will suck the love out of you

do not let another good potential mate slip through the
crack of your insecurities

don't get distracted by potential

do not lose your future due to the mistakes of your past
do not miss destiny while reminiscing over history
spend more time looking at your future than your past

from one queen to another

you deserve to take responsibility of your healing.
and when the universe speaks, you listen.
you will not attract anything that is not meant for you.
i love you.

sis

let that hurt go
but never forget what it taught you

stop your pity party and do the work that it takes to change
your life

if you are not putting in the work then you have no need to
complain
you are the author of your own life
nothing just "happens" to you

navigate through the bad days

i am not here for the pity party
do yourself a favor and lift yourself up

sis
find who you were before him

you will not be able to secure the bag until you secure
your emotional well-being

check yourself before you wreck yourself

———

queen

stop giving up on the person you are becoming

never confuse your soulmate with your lesson learned

self-respecting women do not tolerate bull

stop blaming people for breaking your heart when you
control who you give your energy to

you are the only one not putting yourself first

———

your desire to rise up must be greater than your desire to
get off of the ground and stop being a door mat

don't be angry at other people for doing what you should
have done for yourself

   _____

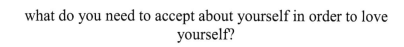

what do you need to accept about yourself in order to love yourself?

unity

to my sisters reading

do not allow your past to determine your future
where you are is not where you will always be.
our healing work should equip the next generation
so that our daughters
baby cousins
nieces
won't have to repeat our mistakes

pouring from an empty cup

we are all a work in progress.
no one can imagine what you have been through or may be
going through at this moment.
please be sure to reach out if you need help, sis.
depression strangled me
until i had absolutely nothing left.

what happens when the sun goes down?
do you love yourself?
are you happy with your choices?

____

never allow anyone to make you feel that you are too
difficult to love

measure how much you are giving out
do not serve from an empty cup

not every woman goes through the ideal life path
of being born, loved, and nurtured properly

not all women are raised to be protected
and reminded of their beauty
but
every woman is predestined to be a queen
even if she could not afford the ability to take the ideal path

even if you are broken
you are no less of a queen

just because your path has been challenging doesn't mean
you have not been a queen all along
you were a queen before you realized it

reclaim your crown and speak

———

SPEAK

in actuality
when people don't express themselves
they die
an unpleasant death
one day
one week
one piece
at a time

SPEAK is in no way designed to bring shame or harm to anyone. I own everything that happened to me and in the words of Anne Lamott, "if people wanted me to write warmly about them, they should have behaved better." Moreover, if you avoid conflict to keep peace, you start a war inside yourself. Here lies my truths, no matter how painful the truths have been. My intent is not to become a bestseller. My intent is to reach the person that needs to hear and read this most.

When healing happened for me, I could no longer keep my mouth shut. The fire within began to spread like fire in a burning forest. I had put in a lot of healing work; formed a solid sisterhood, attended women's healing retreats, and went through each portal of *Sacred Woman* by Queen Afua with the help of Sebayt Queen Dr. Neith's *Sacred Medicine Woman* course. With Queen Neith's support through each portal, I learned to open my throat chakra in order to give a voice to all of the things that I buried. SPEAK was a part of my manifestation because I soon realized that what I lost in the process of healing, was my voice. It became muffled by being embarrassed by my own story. However, through unwinding, unbreaking and creating SPEAK, I gave wings to my pain and let it fly.

When Wounds Speak, You SPEAK.

Someone's breakthrough is locked up in that testimony that you are too afraid to tell. This is why you need to
SPEAK!

Knowing how many women are affected by pain and won't speak up, destroys me. All of the dying that I have to do just so someone in my shoes can live, I will gladly give my life. Honesty is sometimes the hardest thing to bring to the table. Before I started writing my truth, I constantly ignored how much healing I still needed to do. I initially felt like people would look at me differently, but the pain was slowly killing me as I continued to ignore the need to write it out. Now, the allure of freedom is far more important than exposing myself to anyone. It is my desire that when another Queen looks in the mirror after reading SPEAK, she will accept this as my attempt to give her something better. I am extremely transparent, and you can see my truth if you look hard enough.

Think about the concept of a wound. Do wounds heal faster when covered or uncovered?

Scientifically, it is said that a **covered** wound heals faster than an **uncovered** wound. Now I am no scientist, but I have learned from experience that covered wounds are *still* wounds, and covered wounds do not miraculously get better as you grow older.

Over the years I have learned the vital importance of speaking my truth, speaking my peace, and generally speaking up for myself no matter what the circumstance may be and regardless of who may be on the receiving end. When someone hurts my feelings, I SPEAK. If my boss offends me, I SPEAK. When my significant other makes me uncomfortable, I SPEAK. Speaking is one of the most important and most dreaded forms of communication. Thus, the five-step plan that I have put together in this book has ordered my steps and given me the divine powers that I needed to free myself. You see, what tried to kill me, actually reinvented me through my ability to SPEAK. I hope that it does the same for you.

The *S* in SPEAK represents Separation.

Life taught me that your elevation will require
Separation.

I remember the severe depressed state I was in and how much it pained me to exist after learning that my college sweetheart openly started a new relationship while he and I were dating. I was sitting in English class one Tuesday afternoon, and my friend at the time started sending multiple photos to my cell phone of my boo-thing holding hands with a not so strange face; a woman who he assured me on multiple occasions was his best-friend and sister. Needless to say, at that moment, my self-esteem cracked inside of my body. I felt as though my life ended as I scrolled through the photos. We were over two years invested into our relationship and rather than him admitting that he was unhappy with me, he allowed me to discover that he moved on in the worst way. I began to feel inferior.

Separation is the first aspect of my acronym SPEAK. You see, separating from my relationship actually became the turning point for my breakthrough. I was able to spend time alone with myself and during my most idle moments, I began to discover my highest and best self through separation and meditation. I realize that there is love in holding on and there is true love in letting go. I soon learned that a lot of my problems were self-inflicted wounds that derived from negative self-talk. I found that I had stopped growing, stopped setting goals, and grew complacent after what I thought was a heartbreak. Through separation, though, I learned that God will sometimes break your heart to save your soul. Separation taught me to analyze myself and see that I still had a lot of healing to do. I was still hurting from my past. I suffered from abandonment issues. I learned that I was in an unhealthy relationship with myself and it took me to realize it through a toxic relationship. Separation allowed me to recognize my pattern of choosing unsuitable and emotionally unavailable partners. I used to allow people to trample over my personal boundaries. I went along with things that I did not feel comfortable with just to please others. I used to be an over-giver. Yet, I was required to get rid of people who I never imagined living without. On the bright side, getting rid of toxic relationships helped me to understand that separation is absolutely necessary for healing.

Before the Creator can elevate you and set you apart, there are some things that you will need to separate yourself from. Distractions do not look like distractions until they finish distracting you. This means you may have to cut off some family members, you may have to cut off some friends, and you may have to end relationships that are not mutually beneficial to you. Separate from anyone who is not dedicated to your highest and best well-being. The people who refuse to grow and change must all be left behind until they are ready to catch up. Never be afraid to separate from those toxic things and people because when you do, the Universe will begin to take you further than you already were. There will always be separation before elevation. Be humble and let it occur.

I began to fully accept that separation was necessary after people in my life started rejecting me left and right and removing themselves from my life. I literally came home one day and my closest friend at the time had packed all of her bags and moved out of our two-story apartment without a letter, text message, an apology, or even a goodbye. There were no words! I came home from work that evening and was left to pick myself up, as well as pick up bills that were left behind, without a forewarning. But what I thought would be one of the most difficult times of my life during my senior year of college, actually gave me the freedom that I needed. My best friend of 20 years texted me one day to inform me that she thought it would be best if we kept our friendship at a minimum, due to us having different spiritual beliefs. Needless to say, through both encounters, my prayers were secretly being answered. The Most High had been busy removing toxic people from my life in an attempt to help me grow mentally and spiritually.

Truth be told, I was blessed with the space that I needed in order to grow. I was always dedicated to my friends' highest being. I was so focused on ensuring that I handled them with priority, while oftentimes I neglected being kind to myself and being my own best friend. I rarely made time for myself; to allow myself to grow and heal the way I needed without their input and influence. I can recall myself often dimming my own light to make their lights shine. I would shove myself into different social settings, thinking and believing that I had to conform to their beliefs to be accepted. I was wrong.

Throughout my life, most people thought that me valuing my personal space and peace made me selfish or a bad friend. (If you're an only child, I suppose you may understand where I am coming from.) My childhood was relatively separated from siblings, as I was my mother's only child. Thus, people seemed to gravitate toward me relatively easily. At times I struggled to say "no" to going out with certain people who craved my company. I did not quite understand the power of my "no." The moment I began relying solely on my spirit, I began to save myself from heartaches and worry. Through this period of separation, I began reflecting on myself and I began to realize that maybe the friends and guys of my past weren't so bad after all. I realized that I was just as much of the problem as they were. I had to check myself to understand that I was also a toxic person. Being a toxic person did not make me less worthy, but it motivated me to fix the problem -- and that was me.

Separation revealed unacknowledged emotions inside of me and I began to realize that the emotions kept coming up because it was left up to me to address those that I tried hard to bury. When you don't acknowledge your feelings and accept something about yourself, it is a sign that deep down, you don't love yourself enough to change. You will never find true peace with those around you. Through separation, I forced myself to learn how to truly and deeply love and accept myself for who I was, and my feelings for what they were.

Separating myself, (unplugging from social media and doing spiritual exercises) reassured me that I had not been living my best life after all. I realized that being Twitter and Facebook famous meant absolutely nothing when I had not taken the time to cater to myself and inner stand my life's purpose. The power of separation saved my life.

As you will discover through SPEAK, I was on the brink of literally ending my own life. A mental institution became my place of residence after literally *driving myself crazy*. I often say jokingly (because it is the story of my life) that, "You can go crazy, just make sure you come back."

I was in bad shape. Yet, I continued posting on social media like all was well, and I was far from wellness. There is an old African Proverb that reads, *"When there is no enemy within, the enemies outside will not harm you."* I was my own worst enemy before I learned to SPEAK. The more I separated myself, the more self-aware I became. I needed time to myself and I also needed to give space to others who I quickly discovered were no longer a part of my life's purpose. Separating from others is okay. Please do not demonize separation. It is what allowed me to do the necessary self-work that I needed to begin healing from my past. I have learned that you must not continue walking alongside the wrong people and still expect the Universe to favor you. By separating yourself, you may walk alone physically, but the Most High is always with you in spirit. Set yourself apart and prepare for your elevation.

"When God is ready for you to move, He will make your situation uncomfortable." **Germany Kent**

...and boy was I uncomfortable in the Psychiatric Ward. Here is where I was able to vividly see the importance of Prayer.

P in SPEAK represents Prayer Affirmations.

A wise woman prays.

It is necessary to **pray** for yourself while releasing your emotional distress to the Most High. After I began separating myself, I knew that I was ready for elevation. I was tired of being shut in my room, depressed, and watching the world outside of me move on. I did not know how to close the gap between where I was and where I wanted to be in life. I began to pray and recite positive affirmations to set myself apart for divine elevation, as The Most High began elevating me to higher places through meditation. During meditation, The Most High revealed the need to SPEAK about the things that were designed to destroy me.

I strongly believe that prayer affirmations led me to sit in high places and now, nothing is bringing me down. Prayer revealed that I had been emotionally paralyzed and was desperately needing the Creator to wheel me out. The scar on my left thigh let me know that things were serious. I don't know how to explain where the mark came from, but it was deep and showed up in the form on an "X". I was devastated the morning that I woke up in the psychiatric hospital. I actually developed the acronym SPEAK a few months after being released. Immediately afterward, I wanted to remove the muzzle from my mouth and SPEAK about the wounds that I endured which led me there. I previously kept quiet about a lot of things, but this sparked a desire to share what had happened to me with other women who suffered in silence.

I was unsure how women would receive me. Me being the 'token child' of my family -- the first to graduate college and obtain a bachelor's degree, to having the 3rd highest GPA for African American women in my high school graduating class, as well as graduating college as an honor graduate (Summa Cum Laude). How could I share with my peers that I had a nervous breakdown and was hospitalized for seventeen long days? So many people looked up to me and I was embarrassed about my wounds. After being released from the hospital, I remained in my room for several days, weeks, and even months until I learned to increase my prayer and meditation life. I started affirming Jeremiah 29:11. This verse reassured me that there is nothing that I have endured that was meant to be in vain. Thank you Mama A.

I believed that God would use me to heal others someday. I began to affirm that my life would be a platform for other sisters. I only hoped that I went through the things I went through, just so that my sisters, daughters, and my

SPEAK tribe wouldn't have to. I don't look like what I've been through. It was through prayer that I learned to release pain and suffering. I realized the need to release every problem that I carried or tried hard to control. I knew that the Most High would see me through some of the most trying times in my life. I also realized that this was all necessary for me to grow.

From that day going forward, every toxic person that has attempted to hinder me from going to the next level of prosperity, has had to get out of my life.

I suggest in engaging in the power of affirmations:

For starters, repeat the following affirmation to yourself daily: *I release all relationships that do not mutually benefit me. I release everything that I no longer need. I am willing to release everyone who impedes my growth. I release everything that gets in the way of my healing. I love myself. I deserve the best of everything. Anything that is not the best must be evicted from my life, NOW.*

The *E* in SPEAK represents Energy.

Check your energy!

Certain people and their toxic energy can prevent you from elevating. Pay close attention to who your energy increases and decreases around. Negative energy is harmful in many ways. If you are surrounded by negative energy that is coming from a coworker, family member, partner, or friend, you must learn to protect yourself against their negativity without engaging. Surround yourself with people who recharge your energy. Oftentimes, we willingly becomes hosts to those that carry negative energy because a part of us feels like the person is unable to carry their own load. We take on other people's *junk* because we desire to protect them, to heal them and relieve their burdens to make them happy. In actuality, what this does is leave us drained.

You may begin feeling depressed and fatigued. However, you have to check your personal energy immediately to ensure that you are not moved. It is okay to respond to their problems, but do not *react.* Think of who you may be willingly allowing to drain your energy. Yes, it's usually the first person who pops into your mind. When this individual swarms you with their negative thinking, understand that it is okay to listen to their problems as a friend. But it is more important for you to focus on solutions and not just problems. Avoid their drama and set healthy friendship boundaries. Immediately take control of the conversation and help your friend speak in a positive light. When people ask me "what's wrong," I redirect them to "what's right." By responding with what's *right* in my life, I shift my focus from the things that are temporarily going wrong, to highlight everything that is presently going *right.*

I became very stingy with who and what I gave my energy to. When you give your energy to something, it expands and grows. Learn to pay no energy and instead, starve negativity until it dies. Energy is valuable so we must stop giving it to people who are undeserving. Evaluate your relationships and release one-sided relationships. Surround yourself with people who add value to your life.

A few ways that I learned to protect my energy when I became swarmed with negative thinking bees was to focus on solutions and not problems. I avoid drama and set necessary boundaries, denying access to my energy. When you value yourself, you do not give your energy away. I can proudly say that I no longer give my energy away for free. I have placed high value on my energy, and it is my duty to protect my inner peace.

Understand that it is your duty to take care of yourself. It is not your duty to fix everyone and everything. Again, it is okay to respond, but you must never *react*.

My suggestion for you is to repeat the following affirmations when you begin to feel a shift in your energy:
I am free from negative energy drainers.
I have created a safe space for my energy to thrive.
I protect my peace at all times.
My energy is completely mine and it is my responsibility to keep it positive.
I only allow positive energy to flow through me.
I break free from negative people, negative places, and negative things.

It took a lot of deprogramming, spending time alone, and seeking answers from the Most High to learn how to speak life into myself without having to count on others to keep me alive spiritually. Through SPEAK I learned to never place my happiness into someone else's hands. It is important to learn to check your personal energy and celebrate every little thing about yourself in order to truly conquer who you are. In those moments when I did not feel that I could keep moving, I found resilience in sitting naked in the mirror and speaking positive affirmations. Some of my favorites were:

I choose to move forward.
I love myself.
I love the woman that I am becoming.
I am releasing hurt today.
I am not giving up.

I am beautiful.
I am kind.
I am out-Telligent.
I am loved.
I will speak.
What I am is enough.
What I have is enough.
Who I am is enough.
I am enough.

I realized that the more I was around people who were not dedicated to my highest being, I began to absorb their energy. I allowed people to dump their love and family, divorce, and even their financial burdens on me. In this, I learned that people can be extremely draining. At some point, you must learn to say no and refrain from being the person who allows people to dump their energy onto you. If anything, it is draining. You are not a dumpster and you do not need to hold their waste and junk. Learn to separate your assets from your liabilities. Stand firm in positivity and protect your energy, always.

"If the environment that you are in does not acknowledge your anointing, remove yourself. Negative mitigating forces know who you are and plan to implement. You have to have a plan for your life." -Sebayt Queen Dr. Neith Hetshepsut Ma'at

The *A* in SPEAK represents Acknowledgement.

Acknowledge your pain.

It is vital that we acknowledge when we are hurt so that we are able to depart from a world of shame and doubt to live permanently in a world of peace. Set an intention to accept full responsibility for where you currently are in life; physically, mentally, emotionally, and spiritually.

Now, there is no need for self-loathing because pitying yourself does not lead to a satisfying life. It is, however, important to acknowledge your pain. What are you feeling at the moment? Where did those feelings stem from? Fall in love with the way you feel! Sit down with your pain and have some tea. When pain knocks at my door, I welcome it each time. We sit down and I listen as pain teaches me everything that I need to know about myself. Pain is meant to cleanse you. You have to let it in because if you don't, it will knock harder and become louder. So, let it in and unpack the emotional baggage, but do not let it overstay its welcome. Once the pain is finished teaching you, walk it to the door, and command it to leave so that you can welcome peace.

It is important to refrain from becoming overly critical of yourself. It is perfectly okay to acknowledge your weaknesses, but always celebrate your strengths. Accept your past because it is not bad or wrong. Your mistakes are not failures. Learn to look at your mistakes as the footprints that led you to healing, learning, and personal growth.

For beginners, one way to acknowledge pain is to write a letter to yourself. You have been through so much and you must address you -- the one who knows everything that you have been through and felt all of your hurt and pain. Writing the letter will allow you to acknowledge how you feel. It is important to not bury your pain because it will always find its way back to the surface. Write about the hardships you've overcome, and all the goals that you have accomplished. Also be sure to include all of the lives that you have touched and all of the positive connections you have made. Keep your letter close by, review it frequently, and add to it as often as needed. By doing this, you are reminded that where you currently are is not where you will always be. This will allow you to see that where you have been, what you have overcome, cannot deter you from who you are becoming.

Finally, when you have mastered the ability to acknowledge your hurt, learn to let go of the things you have no control over. You must shift your energy to what you can control and release everything that is beyond your control. Some things that you can control are your thoughts, feelings, emotions, your peace, your diet, physical well-being, and your self-acceptance. Honey, by the time I realized the importance of acknowledging my pain and accepting the things that I've been through. I discovered that I had drawn so far away from myself and had been trying to find my way back ever since. I understood that where I was at the time was not my final destination. Where I am now is not where I will always be.

Past regrets can prevent us from practicing self-acceptance. Please forgive yourself and move on. Whether you had an abortion, had your dream car repossessed, got denied into the school of your dream, or failed a class (all of which has happened to me), it is important to learn from the mistake, make an effort to grow, and accept the past that you cannot change.

Regardless of anything, you need to be the person that you look up to most. Do not feel guilty for starting again. Healing will be the greatest yet most difficult time of your life, but you have to SPEAK through it and commit to your decision to heal. Healing for me meant surrendering from one-sided relationships and ridding myself of toxicity. It is important to acknowledge the toxicity in your own life and discover what tools to heal work best for you. Make an effort to visualize your highest and best self that lies deep within. Take a moment to take your mind off of present suffering and dig within to discover the wisdom that already lies within you. By visualizing where you are going, you will promote healing within. You see, the key to healing is understanding that failure is a part of your human experience. The sooner that you understand this, the sooner you   unlock   your   door   to   freedom.

The *K* in SPEAK represents Know.

Know your worth.

Oftentimes, we get off track and we forget who we are. I believe that in being "lost," you have the ability to truly discover yourself and the moment that you discover yourself, you discover your self-respect. Self-respect is the most crucial aspect of your life. If you do not know how to appreciate yourself and your value, you cannot expect another human being to do so. Please do not expect anyone to love or respect you if you don't know your worth. Please understand that your life is too valuable to maintain toxic friendships, relationships, and partnerships — and yes, this includes your job. I used to accept poor managed jobs and relationships, along with toxic friendships, because at the time, I did not know my worth and I did not understand that I deserved better. You need to know how to only connect with people that make you happy and motivate you to grow. A lack of knowing your worth often results in self-destruction. In the end, you will always have self-respect to rely on. How you feel about yourself affects every single aspect of your life.

If you do not respect yourself then you will not take care of yourself the way that you should. You cannot allow people to treat you poorly and if they do, you must recognize your worth and distance yourself from negativity. Others cannot negatively influence your opinion of yourself, as this will only dim your light. You must love, approve, and respect yourself before anyone else can.

As humans, we often accept the love that we think we deserve. Thus, self-love, and self-esteem, and self-respect play hand in hand with one another. Self-love is the appreciation for oneself that stems from our physical, mental, emotional, and spiritual growth. Self-love is a dynamic force that shows compassion for ourselves as we get in tune with our life purpose and values. Self-esteem gives you the confidence to succeed. Without it you are simply placing limitations on yourself. Self-respect is fluid when you know your worth. It allows you to take pride in who you are and what you have to offer.

You and only you are responsible for your destiny. Life is not worth living if you spend it hating who you are. This stifles any progress you hope to make. Once you *know* that you are an asset, you will stop making the terrible mistake of not being comfortable and happy with who you are. How can you truly learn to appreciate others if you do not appreciate yourself? This is fundamental to personal growth.

Know your worth.
Know who you are,
Know whose you are.
Know where you are headed in life.
Know that where you are now is not where you will always be.
Know your ability to move forward.
Know your strengths and weaknesses.
Know your worth.

Know your worth.
Please darling, know your worth.

Now that you have the tools, you are ready to SPEAK.

WHAT HAPPENS WHEN WE SPEAK

I've had the opportunity to talk two women out of abortion. Not because I did not support their decisions, but because I know what the aftermath feels like. I know what it's like to cry about the same thing 10 years straight, to feel as though your world was ripped away from you and the emotional aftermath that will remain with you until you heal. I sat next to my close friend in the abortion clinic as she contemplated on whether or not she was going to go through with it. I prayed hard while we were sitting there, and she looked at me after two hours and said "I can't do it. Let's go." And we left.

As I learn to heal and let go of my personal trauma identity, I understand the importance of not being silent about pain. And just because you did something wrong in the past does not mean that you cannot advocate against it in the present.

Author Queen

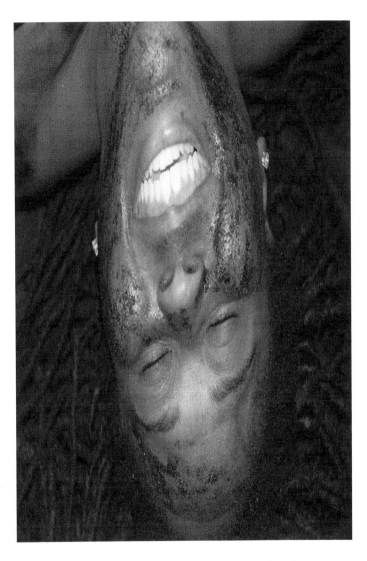

silence can sometimes be a woman's loudest cry

abortion is one of the hardest things i have ever been
through
but you must share your story
even when your voice is shaking
even when you know people will judge you
it has been just over 10 years
i had been badly traumatized from a series of very
toxic relationships when i was younger
emotional turmoil and did not know how to process it
spent twelve hours per day crying and throwing up

———

fragile

as a child, i developed a need for a man to love me more
than my father and step father
years of hurting happened
months of healing is in process
timing is everything
you cannot rush a beautiful wound to heal
accept who you are
where you are
the unpleasant confrontations that you face along the way
helps you flourish
i am not afraid of my truths anymore

i cannot be everything to everyone if i am nothing to
myself

my past was practice
the mistakes i made along the way
will keep me on the right track today

even if i fall today, my truth will pick me up again.
when i am afraid to speak
i speak
when my voice trembles
i speak

testimony

let me stand as a testimony
to what they have done to me
to us
my wounds will not be silent
i'm just a love machine and i did not work for anybody but
you.

_____

dear reader:

the love that you desire to give to someone else
is the love that you must give to yourself
you cannot pour from an empty cup
there is no need to try to make another individual happy
when you yourself still have mountains of happiness to
climb

―――

write until your fingers bleed
write until your knuckles lock
write your truth
speak your truth
you have permission to speak
remove your muzzle and set yourself free
speak for you and speak for me
do not be silent about your pain
you owe you
speak
speak for you
speak for him
speak for freedom
do not remain silent about your pain
please, speak up
now

remember that when you speak, your actions must match
the words that are coming out of your mouth

dear future fiancé,

i had high hopes for you
and i still do
please be able to love my naked soul
before you make love to my naked body

———

it seems as though men are not taught to love
men are taught survival

please raise kings to know and understand balance
love and survival go hand in hand
in matrimony

you can't have one without the other in a sacred union

_____

i have felt the effects of my mistakes many times
and wondered if life is worth to have another chance
but the truth is that I would not be here today if it was not
for my ability to SPEAK
and if you learn one thing today
learn this

you are not who they have made you
you are not the mistakes you made
you are exactly what you make yourself from this day
forward
and it is never too late to start again

——

i am still breathing as i learned to crawl my way out.
i lost myself to each one of them—
gave love with little in return and sometimes none at all.
but i learned from my mistakes
and i speak so that others won't have to be afraid to own up
to who they once were

_____

never love anyone more than you love yourself
it is not fair to you

i am the voice of women who are scared to speak up
do not be ashamed of you

i speak because slave women had no voice as they were
raped
speak for the women who had no voice when their children
were taken and sold
speak for women whose sons are murdered
i speak because children are told that what happens in
mama's house stays in mama's house
but children need help too

———

set boundaries for what you will accept

do not over extend yourself

fast forward

i wrote speak from my soul
i shed a few tears as i wrote
you may not understand it all but
thank you
dear reader
for reading.

from the heart

S.P.E.A.K.

I speak because it heals others as I heal myself
I speak because I choose not to run from my problems but
face the problem head on
I speak because I conquer everything that was destined to
destroy me
I speak because I once was living in fear, but I am no
longer afraid to show up for myself
I speak because I was hurt in relationships, but I
commanded my voice to get through
I speak because I did not get what I deserved from the
world through silence, so I learned to create my own voice
I speak because when I could not find comfort in others, I
created comfort and security within
I speak because I embrace my imperfections and nothing
that I have gone through can be used against me to destroy
me
I speak because it empowers me
I speak because God will sit at my right hand and make my
enemies my foot stools
I speak because I almost gave up
I speak because speaking saved my life
I speak because it enables me to keep standing tall
I speak because speaking heals wounds and I have the right
to speak on how I feel

Let go of what happened and command your voice to
SPEAK.

I am thankful for my struggle because without it, I would
not have stumbled across my strength to speak

to you –

to the one who believes i have something worth reading,
the one who will share my words, remember that your
words matter too.

command the voice you have been given to make a positive
change in the world
my voice alone can only fill one room
but our voices together will make the heavens roar

SPEAK

SPEAK as you forgive yourself
SPEAK as you forgive your family
SPEAK as you lavish in your wholeness
SPEAK as you accept your reality
SPEAK to protect your energy
SPEAK so that you calm down
SPEAK to find light in the darkness
SPEAK as you remember your worth
SPEAK as you trust your path
SPEAK to balance your emotions
SPEAK manifestations and then go get what you just
prayed for
SPEAK so that your gifts are recognized
SPEAK until you find your worth
SPEAK your living truth
SPEAK Queen,
SPEAK King
SPEAK.

Acknowledgements

SPEAK would not have been possible without the love and support from family and close friends. I am indebted to The Goddess Network to Networth, the administrators, Alexis Jaleena, Angie Harris, and Meymoona Freeman who have been supportive of my career as an authorpreneur and who worked actively to provide me with the Goddess Network funds to pursue this goal.

I give thanks for Sebayt Queen Dr. Neith for assisting me with my healing journey. Dua, Ankh & Mer for helping me first recognize the traumas that I worked extremely hard to bury and assisting me as a Master Teacher through each sacred portal. I wish every woman my age had a Sebayt Queen Dr. Neith in her life. Dua for teaching me that A Wise Woman Builds Her Home, and a Foolish Woman Tears It Down with Her Own Hands (Proverbs). Thank you for holding me accountable for my actions as well as my inactions. Dua for always being patient with me and being an all-around great healer. I am grateful to my Grand Mut and Sacred Sorors with whom I have had the pleasure to work during this and other healing projects. Each of you provided me extensive personal guidance and taught me a great deal about healing and life in general. Dua Sebayt Queen Dr. Neith, Grand Mut, SNT Ntrs, SSs, and SAs for being women of authority who are under authority.

Nobody has been more important to me in the pursuit of self-care than the founder of SisterCare Alliance, Anana Harris Parris. She is the ultimate role model whose guidance is with me in whatever I choose to pursue. I wish to thank Attorney Mawuli Davis and Attorney Robert Bozeman for first giving me a chance to work the job of my dreams as an intern. Thank you for being great role models and thank you for believing in me. Thank you to my loving and supportive mother, step-father, and grandmother for giving me a voice and allowing me to always be myself while respecting me and giving loving correction through my discovery walk. Thank you to my aunt Natalie who told me "Baby, if you have to cry everyday...cry. But the hurt will pass."

Thank you Nia, The Literary Revolutionary, for providing unending inspiration and helping me jumpstart my career as an authorpreneur. I would like to send a special thank you to my father because although you were incarcerated for 11 years of my life, you wrote many letters to me, of which I still have and keep near and dear to my heart. No matter the distance, the love kept us close. I remember you often sending me what you considered "homework" and asked me to do it and mail it back to you. I give thanks for your time served which molded you into one of the greatest fathers with a pure heart of Gold. I give thanks for your patience with me, showing me unconditional love, and allowing me to be who I am at ease.

About the Author

I am Author Queen, Lattifa Bryant. I am a SPEAK Authorpreneur who encourages women to command their voices to speak freely about internal pain (such as childhood trauma, relationship trauma, emotional abuse, abortion, miscarriage, and negative-self talk). I am the owner and founder of SPEAK, a radical approach to self-love. I developed this five step plan moments after I found myself wearing a spiritual muzzle on my mouth which forced me into silence about childhood traumas, my experience with depression, and emotional abuse. Through my five-step plan, my goal is to offer women a better approach to owning their trauma identity. SPEAK aids women with healing through expanding the importance of separation, which is required for elevation, prayer affirmations, energy check ins, self-acceptance, and ultimately teaching women to know their worth. SPEAK does not promise to repair your brokenness. The SPEAK method is not a magic trick that you snap your fingers to and KA-POW: BOOM! "You're healed." Oh no. SPEAK *does* promise to give you a proven set of tools that if used, will give you the power that you need to use your voice, even if it shakes. SPEAK is a tool that I developed to heal my inner-self, and I hope that through SPEAK, you muster up the courage to do the same. You are worth fighting for!

I graduated Summa Cum Laude from Georgia State University (Go Panthers) and received my bachelor's degree in African American Studies and English in 2016. Studying African American studies changed my perspective on so many things! I began to fall in love with the way brown people think, feel, and act in an attempt to understand how they (we) deal with trauma. It was essential for me to get to the root of the matter as I engaged myself in the complexities of African American male and female relationships, and enslaved vs slave owner relationships. Through my studies, I realized that there was a pattern throughout history that proved that black women were thought to feel no pain, according to historical experiments that were performed on black women without anesthesia. In fact, one of the most thought-provoking stories is of a masked woman called Escrava Anastacia, an enslaved African woman who was raped repeatedly and forced to wear an iron mask for the rest of her life as a form of slave punishment. She was forced to live with the mask, and only allowed to remove it once a per day to eat. After a few years, the metal from the mask became poisonous, and she died of tetanus. My work is heavily influenced by the legend of Escrava Anastacia, and many other African American women who were deprived of their voices. I am not my sister's keeper: I am my sister. She, like many other women, was forced to be silent about her pain. But I declare that the lives of each woman that I come across, regardless of racial background or ethnicity, will be empowered to remove her muzzle and speak freely about pain.

I have worked on a global scale as the secretary and treasurer of the Georgia State National Black Law Student Association Chapter. I am also the recipient for the Street Scholarship, as well as the 2015 Kwame Ture community service award, granted from the Department of African American Studies at Georgia State University. I am also a member of the Delta Epsilon Iota Honors society.

As a published author, poet, and mentor for Girls SPEAK, I am considered a multi-faceted woman. I have received many praises and many thanks for my work empowering others to SPEAK, as I continuously share my own human experience through creative expression and poetry.

58850230R00146

Made in the USA
Columbia, SC
27 May 2019